THE RISING STORM

THE
RISING
STORM

Bert H. Wallace

Pentland Press, Inc.
United States of America

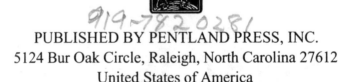

919-782-0281

PUBLISHED BY PENTLAND PRESS, INC.
5124 Bur Oak Circle, Raleigh, North Carolina 27612
United States of America

ISBN 1-57197-000-2
Library of Congress Catalog Card Number: 95-68077

Copyright © 1995 Bert H. Wallace

All rights reserved, which includes the right to reproduce this book or portions thereof in any form whatsoever except as provided by the U.S. Copyright Law.

Printed in the United States of America

To Vivian, John, Benjamin and David

ONE
The Headless Statue

New Year's Eve, 1918, midnight, seven weeks after the end of World War I. Two shots rang out. Then the shattering of a heavy stone object. I woke up crying. Aunt Emmy rushed into my bedroom to pacify me while everybody else ran heedlessly into the icy street to find out what was happening.

Soon they found out and quickly returned to the house, not only to escape the bitter cold, but also to be the first to report what at this time was still largely unconfirmed. My brother Theo sought out Aunt Emmy who had been sitting on my bed talking softly to me but who, nevertheless, was terribly eager to find out. It was many years later that I discovered the reason for her curiosity.

I was a chance listener as my brother Theo related to our Aunt Emmy the story of how a well-known young man, Isidor Heil, who came from an honorable Catholic family and, of all crazy things, was our devout housemaid Bertha's brother, had gotten drunk during the New Year's revelries at Rieser's Inn. Goaded by a couple of communist leaders in our village, he picked up his army rifle, aimed it at the head of the Jesus statue that stood in the center of the church plaza and with two shots, tore off the Lord's head so that it came crashing down on the statue's stone pedestal.

Of all the unthinkable things that could happen in this Catholic village, this was perhaps the most unthinkable, especially since the perpetrator came from a god-fearing and respected Catholic family.

Until this moment, Isidor Heil had undoubtedly been the village's favorite son, handsome and strong, so that even my father admitted grudgingly that should there ever be a wrestling contest in the village, he would yield to no one except "perhaps" to Issy. Presently, Isidor panicked as the full consciousness of his misdeed dawned on him through the mist of his inebriation.

He ran home as fast as he could, and he was easily the fastest runner in the village, packed up a suitcase and whatever money he could lay his hands on and rushed to the railroad station to catch the midnight train to Hamburg. Afterward, whenever the folks talked about this event in the village, they always finished the story with the ominous words "he took off in night and fog."

Having committed the ultimate sin, he could sin no more. In fact, to many youngsters, he became their role model-in-absentia, so to speak, their saint or superman, depending on their ideological preference, and he was assumed to be living a life of everlasting happiness in the far off and anonymous city of Hamburg.

Many years later, when the dark clouds of German fascism engulfed Europe, Isidor's and my life chanced to cross one another several times in some miraculous manner and despite the difference in age of almost twenty years, I had the great pleasure and comfort to count him as one of my best friends, a most beautiful person.

However, for quite a number of years, Issy was not allowed to show his face in his native village, much to the sorrow of his sister who had long forgiven him and many of his friends. As we learned later, he had found a good job as a carpenter in a shipyard in a suburb of Hamburg. There he made a decent living and married a lovely woman but their marriage was not blessed with children.

But, of course, we are rushing the progress of history.

TWO
Earliest Recollections

Nowadays, when you visit the village of Flieden in Hesse, you will immediately notice the baroque church built in the middle of the village on one of the numerous plateaus that dot the old thruway between the district capital of Fulda and the metropolis of Frankfurt. At its left, or eastern half, the church plaza is separated from the road by a brick wall about five feet high.

On the other side of the street, a steep mountain road, the Zent, takes off like a giant T and leads you to the newer part of the village. It continues past the old cemetery, then divides into branches that wind up at several hamlets north of the village.

However, more than half a century ago, the center of the village looked somewhat different. In place of that brick wall that girds part of the church plaza now stood the formidable, three story high, hundred and twenty foot long general store of Isaiah Katz, presided over by my father, Baruch Wallach, and my uncle, Nathan Katz. They were assisted in varying degrees by a mix of children from both families, spinster aunts, cousins and employees, all living either in our house, which was an integral part of the general store, or in the Katz house across the street.

In our store you could buy almost anything, except shoes and meat, in mutual deference to the local shoemakers and butchers. As a result of a long-standing symbiotic compact with them they were also our customers. In our store you could buy suits, dresses, coats, or fabrics for them, hats for men and women, haberdashery, kitchen stoves, ovens, bicycles, milk-and-butter separators, furniture, hardware, herring, fish in season, legumes, dried vegetables, sugar, salt, cooking oil, motor oil, axle grease, petroleum, coffee, chocolates, candy, cigarettes, cigars, smoking pipes and pipe tobacco, soap and toilet articles, structural steel, bar stock, steel and copper pipes and fittings, and sheet metal. Even pharmaceuticals were dispensed until government regulations required pharmacists to be certified. In the late twenties we began to sell radios.

Of the five hundred odd families in the village, about half owned small or medium sized farms. There were about six inns, two barbers, two doctors, one midwife, two bakers, three butchers of which one was kosher, a half dozen Jewish cattle-dealers who supplied the butchers with calves, cows, oxen, goats or sheep, occasionally an aged or infertile bull, while the pigs were purchased directly from the local farmers. There were three carpenters, two blacksmiths, three tailors, five small retail stores, one book binder, one or two electricians, two shoemakers in the process of changing over from making shoes-to-order to selling the new mass-produced ones.

There was the mayor lording it over several civil service people. We also had one postmaster, one mailman, one gendarme who got around on bicycle, and a station master with a number of people to help him sell tickets and run the railroad.

In the elegant manse to the east of the church, behind our store, there lived Dr. Winter, the parish priest, widely beloved and respected by everybody for his sense of humor, his humanity and his sincerity, and remembered by me mostly for his receding reddish-blond hair line, his short, beaked nose, his gold-rimmed glasses and his ever-ready smile.

The Flieden Public School had about three hundred fifty students in the mandated seven to fourteen-year-old age group, guided by about ten teachers of varying capabilities and popularities.

There was also a one-room Jewish parochial school, *Herr* Simon Freudenberger holding forth. Since the Jewish community counted fewer than twenty families, the school population, from the first to the eighth grade, usually numbered no more than eight to twelve pupils. Some "classes" consisted of but one or two pupils, or none, a circumstance that made *Herr* Freudenberger's task difficult.

The bulk of the remainder of the population, the working class, commuted to Fulda, about twelve miles from Flieden and worked in factories there.

There was also a small assortment of ne'er-do-wells, wife beaters, and full-time drunks, some of whom spent part of the day sleeping in the gutter, or in jail, depending on the weather.

4

For a village of twenty three hundred, where news and rumors traveled fast, there was surprisingly little whoring going on but that aspect of life was, by consensus, hidden carefully from this preschool-age boy. Indeed, life proceeded in a steady and well-regulated manner.

In this village, too, by the inexorable law of statistics, there was on the average about one death a week, and one birth, and we often watched the funeral services conducted by Dr. Winter from our *Altane* (rear balcony). From there, too, we could watch when little babies were brought there to be baptized.

However, what has engraved itself as the most enduring part upon my memory was the flow of the seasons. Above all, the spring with its short showers and long sunshine produced a swell of lust for life and happiness. The blossoming of the flowers, the apple and cherry trees, the fragrances of the lilies-of-the-valley and the violets, the forget-me-nots along the banks of the stream Fliede, each appearing in their own good time, the scent of fresh earth, the new lettuce beds, all breathed in, in a vague but overpowering way, through the nostrils, the mouth, the pores and even the eyes and ears of a three-year-old boy, all combined to settle once and for all time to come the question of the worthwhileness of life.

How, indeed, could the wonderful months of April, May and June in Flieden be bested by anything in the great wide world?

But the other seasons too had their attractions. In this predominantly Catholic village where life seemed to be so constant, where nothing ever was expected to change, where even the arrival of a new Protestant family was upsetting, some building and rebuilding was nonetheless going on all the time.

Most of this work was done by the homeowners themselves for the reason that hardly anybody had enough money to hire contractors. Piles of bricks, sand and cement were the tell-tale signs of such goings-on. So in any given period of the year, my next-door pal, Yoppe, who topped me by one year, and myself, armed with pails and toy shovels, would dig a tunnel through the sand, invariably representing the great railroad tunnel that ran through the mountain between Flieden and the next railroad stop, Schlüchtern.

At other times, we would construct a magnificent castle for one fairy tale king, or another, in blissful ignorance of the fact that the German people had just kicked out their idiot emperor Willy II for losing the war, or rather, for starting it in the first place.

There were times when Yoppe and I were joined by Trudi and Adolf Schäfer, the children of the village midwife living on the Zent. They were two and three years older than I was, hence, they were people that a four year old would look up to. Despite their considerable seniority, they were gentle with us and never took advantage of their greater size.

Alas, their gentleness was not emulated by their big dog, Rolf. Except for his black nose, he was yellow-haired. He was a mixed breed, part German shepherd, part police dog. The story made the rounds that on the way back from the war, Schäfer encountered a couple of Belgian smugglers shuttling back and forth between the warring lines and making a handsome profit from their illicit trade. He threatened to have them shot but settled instead for their big dog. Rolf got to know us children well. He was mostly gentle with us but there were times when his wild nature would break through.

I was usually invited to spend the Christmas holidays with the Schäfers. Once, I remember going up to their house during Christmas morning and walking through the unlocked door when I realized that everybody was still asleep. I turned around to go back home. Suddenly, there was Rolf fledging his teeth, snarling at me and threatening to jump me, or worse. Now, he was a big dog. In the past, whenever we had met in the presence of a member of the Schäfer family, he would rise on his hind legs and, good-naturedly, give me a dog's hug. At such a moment, I realized that he was almost a foot taller than I was and I had a hard time humoring him in order to get him to climb off me. Now with none of the Schäfers around, he behaved as though I was an intruding stranger. I was scared as hell. Finally, *Herr* Schäfer came out of his bedroom dressed in his nightshirt. He was still half asleep and yawning. He calmly ordered Rolf to lay off me.

Another time, I was running down the Zent, when Rolf tore himself loose from Trudi's leash and came after me in full fury. Before I knew it, he had caught up with me and sank his fangs into my rear. Poor Trudi came running after him to retrieve the leash, but it was too late. Not only had Rolf torn my pants, but he had garnered about a half a cubic inch of my posterior, and that as well as the disinfecting ointment that my worried mother applied immediately, was painful. For years, anybody who was insistent enough to look, noted the dark-fleshed testimonial to this frightening encounter.

It was many years later when Trudi was in her teens, that she was found in a closet with a neighbor's boy and the rumor began to spread in the village that Trudi had become a sort of hands-on, if surreptitious, instructor of sexual practice for the latest crop of village teenagers. However, before I get too far ahead of my story I must tell you something about my pal Yoppe and his family. They were our next door neighbors. Yoppe, a nickname for Joseph, had an older brother who kept very much to himself, and two older sisters. Their father was a carpenter and he used the largest room in the house as his workshop. He was also the church custodian and was entitled to live rent-free in this church-owned house.

I remember that on almost every wall of every room of their house there hung a good-sized, framed print of Jesus. He was easily recognized by his reddish blond curly hair and his watery brown eyes looking dolefully upon the cross that he had to carry.

At that time, all I knew about Jesus was that he had lived in Nazareth and gone through some terrible, incomprehensible suffering until, finally, he was crucified. A life-sized Jesus statue hewn of stone, nailed to a large stone cross which was anchored to a multi-tiered pedestal, stood right in the middle of the church plaza, and all the male passers-by would pull their hats in reverence, while the ladies would make the sign of the cross. The original head of Jesus, a casualty of Isidor Heil's shameful transgression, had long been replaced.

When Yoppe's father came down with tuberculosis and was moved around from one hospital to another until he died, leaving the family destitute, the older son took over his father's custodial job just to keep the use of the house and picked up some occasional carpentry work that was thrown his way. Throughout this trying period, my pal Yoppe would never express his pain, nor let his anger out on me. He was the gentlest person in the village, to the point of self-denial. And he was my pal!

Yoppe's gentleness was truly contagious. I am sure it saved me from developing my father's notorious temper. When our family moved to nearby Fulda in the summer of 1929, when we were both teenagers, we went our separate ways and lost track of each other.

After six decades, while revisiting my native village I heard to my great joy that he had survived the Second World War and was now living in retirement with his family in a nearby spa. I decided to visit him there. The moment that he opened the door, we recognized each other and embraced one another in meaningful silence. Over a cup of coffee, and ringed by his family, we exchanged the main happenings in our lives during those fateful decades.

Another person with whom I had a wonderful relationship at that time was Herman Lotz, the village electrician. A tall, handsome man of about forty, with a black mustache and a delightful sense of humor, he would often come to our store in the wee hours of the evening and mix his own type of grog. Some rum, a shot of vinegar, a few drops of lemon juice and a tablespoon of sugar. Jokingly, he would bend down to me, offer me a sip of his brew, and then break into a short, friendly grin.

When I was about five years old, *Herr* Lotz would take me along to some of the houses where he would install lighting as part of the new post-war electrification program in our area. After Dr. Tölle's building across the street, ours was next in line to have electricity. *Herr* Lotz would patiently explain to me that all lights need two wires and a switch to turn them on and off.

Once, while climbing up a ladder in order to connect the wires to a lamp socket in the ceiling, he was so involved talking to me that he had forgotten to disconnect the fuse. He touched both live wires and was knocked off the ladder. As I rushed frantically up to him he embraced me and said feebly, "Good thing I fell off the ladder, otherwise I would be dead." Surprisingly, he was unhurt. Hermann Lotz was a sort of lefty and, oftentimes, when he came to the store and had gulped down his second glass of grog, he and my father would become involved in an argument about the advantages and disadvantages of the free enterprise system. *Herr* Lotz claimed that it was the rivalries of the capitalist blocks and the greed of the armament kings that had plunged the world into war. My father, on the other hand, told *Herr* Lotz that without capitalists, there would be no jobs and everybody would be on the dole.

Of course none of the arguments ever led to any agreement, but I believe that watching my awe-inspiring father in the same arena with a contestant of similar intelligence helped me develop a saner perspective in my relationship with my father. It did not go as far as to produce the fall of a "child's idol," but it lowered the paternal image by a few healthy notches.

Schoolboy

May 1922, about ten o'clock in the morning. I was all dressed up in a blue sailor suit, standing in the store, surrounded by my parents, my sister Elli, my two brothers, Julius and Theo, Aunt Emmy, and several clerks. We were all waiting for my cousin Erwin Katz from across the street who, at that moment, was being equally admired by his parents, his sisters Lina and Bella, and his brothers Rudi and Walter. The day before, my hair had been cut from a pageboy style to one with a parting, while cousin Erwin's pate was reduced to a bald trim.

For this was the day we were entering first grade of elementary school, the parochial school of our congregation, where *Herr* Simon Freudenberger was the teacher and principal besides which he was also the cantor, preacher, ritual slaughterer and foremost defender of the faith in our village, all rolled together, dispensing these various functions with a considerable touch of mediocrity, but always with the utmost sincerity.

Pretty soon, you would see my brother Theo, me, my cousin Erwin and his sister Bella, in that order, walk, four abreast, down the main thoroughfare and across the stone bridge over the Fliede River. But instead of following that road past Rieser's Inn, we continued straight ahead until we arrived at the Jewish School.

Then, as a symbolic gesture that Erwin and I had reached a milestone in our lives, our two companions handed each of us a long cone-shaped bag wrapped in colorful paper as a present for our first day in school. Once inside, we discovered that it contained an orange, a bar of chocolate and the paraphernalia for performing at our brand-new profession as pupils: a framed slate, lined on one side, two slate pencils, one regular lead pencil, a pencil sharpener and an eraser, the latter items in a pretty wooden box.

Herr Freudenberger received us rather ceremoniously and introduced us to the rest of the students, six or seven in all ranging in age from nine to fourteen, strangely oblivious of the fact that we had known each other all our lives anyway. He then assigned us our seats on the front bench.

Brother Theo and cousin Bella left and at that moment, we realized however vaguely, that we had just changed from an almost totally untrammeled period of playing without a care to a period

9

where, in my father's oft repeated words, we now had to carry out our "bounden duty and responsibility." Although this was still a rather nebulous concept in my six-year-old mind, it nevertheless gave me a rush of butterflies for the first time in my life.

Herr Freudenberger proceeded directly to the business at hand. He asked me if I could tell him the price of one half liter of salad oil, if one liter costs thirty pennies. Since I had sold many a half liter and also many full liters of salad oil in our store, I gave him the answer without flinching. He acknowledged my answer with a grin and followed up asking me how much two times two was. Still riding high on my first triumph, I replied that this was such a simple problem that I wouldn't even honor it with an answer.

I must confess that this wise guy response, while delighting the teacher, did not score any Brownie points with my fellow students. For many years thereafter I had to listen to this story, usually combined with some unflattering comment about my humility.

However, on the whole, I believe that I was rather well liked by the other students. It took no time before the butterflies gave way to a good feeling about myself. I also gained by fending for myself in those thousand and one everyday squabbles among schoolchildren. I had no inclination ever to fall back on my father as some of the sob sisters would do with their fathers or bigger brothers, simply because I feared that my father would immediately have blamed me for having started the dispute. Much later I came to realize that my father would actually defend me like a lion whenever I was myself unable to resolve a fight with one of the village bullies.

Fortunately, there were not many of those in our village. This was also borne out a decade later, when the scourge of fascism of the German variety burst upon the scene, and barely a handful of native Nazis came out of the village closet. While this cold fact in no way saved the remainder of the Jews still living in Flieden from sharing the same horrible fate that befell their brethren in the rest of Europe, the village on the whole, lived through the Nazi horror and the war with a fair degree of its sanity left intact. This assessment, construed many years after the events, takes into account the tremendous deprivations of the populace and the loss of life in the war which, in this village alone, amounted to twice that suffered during the First World War.

It was just about that time that the Great Inflation started.

THREE
Inflation

The victorious allies had levied momentous sanctions of goods and money against Germany. France, in particular, had her hungry eyes set on the vast coal reserves of the Ruhr Valley to be used for the refining of the Alsace-Lorraine iron ore, just as Bismarck had made war against France in 1870 to garner the huge iron ore deposits of Alsace-Lorraine for the exact same purpose of combining the French steel and the German coal under one hat, so to speak, in the latter case, the hat of the Ruhrbarons. Now it was France's turn. When the German miners refused to fill the required quota, the French and Belgian armies occupied the Ruhr Valley and tried to make the German miners work "under the bayonet."

History will record that about twenty years later, Hitler followed a similar dictum. Right at the outset of World War II, he made haste to occupy the iron-rich strip of Belgium and Alsace-Lorraine, settling down in what came to be called the *Sitzkrieg*, in the vain hope that the English would change sides and go with him against the Russians.

Coming back to the first few years after World War I, it was not long before a shortage of goods arose that was even worse than the one that existed toward the end of the war. As the German mint printed more and more money to make up for the huge payments to the allies, the German *Mark* started its historic downslide in value.

In order to save paper, they soon began to print the new values right over the old bills, first ten, then a hundred, then a thousand *Marks* until, by 1923, the One *Mark* bill had one billion printed across its face.

Almost every day a new rate was announced, but in those days before radio came into use, by the time the newspapers reached their readers, often the published rate was already out of date.

I recall very well that on a given day in 1923, Uncle Nathan, who was slowly losing his mind from this never-ending adjustment malaise, asked me to take a briefcase bulging with paper money together with our ever-present payment book to our local post office, so that the postmaster could telegraph the amounts due that day to the respective wholesalers' post offices for prompt payment.

That day, as soon as I entered the post office, Postmaster Maul yelled to me that Uncle Nathan had just called and that I was to return at once to pick up more money since the rate had gone up again.

In our store, we had long ceased posting the ever changing retail prices on the merchandise. Instead, our goods were coded with a base price expressed in the individual letters of the Brazilian state of Pernambuco, where p=1, e=2, etc., and every salesperson knew the daily multiplier. To keep our losses to a minimum, we, together with all the other retailers in the country, had to keep our inventory in short supply. This in turn hurt the wholesalers and manufacturers. Hence, the factories had to lay off a great many workers.

Even for the worker who still had a job, this inflation wreaked havoc with his income. At the beginning of every work week he would be told what his wage would be for that week, and he knew that at the end of that week, on payday, he would be paid the promised nominal value. However, when he went to do his weekly shopping, he found that, once again, he had less spending money than he had the week before.

Into this utterly hopeless situation steps Horace Greeley Hjalmar Schacht, the economic wunderkind of the era. He stabilized the *Mark* at its pre-inflation value. From one day to the next, a billion *Marks* was once again one *Mark*. One dollar which one day was traded for four billion *Marks*, could be bought for the original four *Marks* the next day.

At first, Schacht's scheme was considered ingenious. But soon, there followed a sad awakening. Everybody's lifetime savings were gone. Half the middle class was wiped out. The suicide rate reached an absolute peak. Nobody had anymore money to carry on a decent living, except the large entrepreneurs who still had their capital equipment, and the large banks who still had their credit instruments and to whom everybody owed a lot of money. Since people could not afford to buy much of anything anymore, sometimes not even the bare necessities of life, new factory orders ran down to a snippet, and more millions of workers were laid off and went on the dole.

FOUR
Conflagration

When I was about seven years old, one night around 3 or 4 A.M., there was a tremendous, persistent noise that woke me up with a start, and I immediately rushed to my parents' bedroom. I was surprised to find my two brothers and my sister there, all dressed up as though there was a regular family gathering. Since everybody stared out of the window, I too followed their gaze and there, in utter disbelief, what I beheld was a plume of fire coming out of the Gass house on the Zent.

Since their house stood almost exactly at right angles to ours, high up on the hill about a hundred fifty feet away, with fire coming out from under the near corner of the roof, it looked as though a superhuman colossus was holding up a giant torch that lit up the complex of buildings immediately in front of us. I simply could not understand why just about half the villagers had gathered in the streets around the burning house, all staring toward that plume of fire coming out of that house. It was only then that I looked down to my left and realized that the two barns that had been attached to Dr. Tölle's brick house had already burned to the ground. At that moment, cousin Julius Adler, who was officially an employee of the company and, besides, a factotum for all kinds of family affairs, came into the room and reported that he and two helpers earlier had stationed themselves strategically on our roof and armed with pails filled with water, had extinguished three fires that had started on our roof by some embers and sparks thrown up by the first fire, and that the danger to our house had now passed. I felt ashamed that all that had happened while I had been sleeping and nobody had bothered to wake me up. Fire, floods or wild animals were things that filled my childhood imagery with absolute terror. Presently, I developed a chill and crawled into my mother's bed. I was trembling all over and had goose bumps that did not go away for a half hour.

Soon, the family conversation turned to the question of why, after many hours of the earlier fire, the Gass house started only now to light up. It was known that old man Gass had recently taken out some handsome fire insurance and that started a speculation that would not die soon, that this may be a case of arson. Of course, everybody in the village was well aware that the entire fire department was drunk, cheered on by the notorious boozers Anton and Emil, the Gass's sons, and that the firefighters had hacked parts of the house down even before the flames got there and did their job, just to make sure that the house was going to be a total loss. Interestingly when, after many months of haggling, the insurance company took the Gass family to court and accused them of arson, all the members of the local fire brigade when called as witnesses, pleaded ignorance by reason of intoxication and the insurance company lost its case and had to pay up.

Since Anton and Emil Gass were accomplished carpenters and did most of the rebuilding themselves, soon there stood a new, handsome house next to ours. In addition, they modernized their woodworking machinery and I became their favorite, if only part-time vocational trainee, taking the greatest care never to let on that they were in an almost perpetual state of inebriation. With me they were patient and caring, and woodworking became one of my lifetime hobbies.

Many years later, my cousin Bella related the story which had then been making the rounds in Flieden, that Frau Gass was so pious that once, when somebody suggested to her in a tactful manner that she should take a bath once in a while, she protested that taking off one's clothes was a mortal sin. No wonder her sons had become alcoholics.

FIVE
Soccer

It was about that time that the soccer bug took hold of us. My pal Yoppe who, if you remember, lived in the house next to ours, Adolf, the son of the village midwife, and Willie Gass and his brother Hermann, cousins of Anton and Emil, whose family owned Vogel's Inn on the far side of the church plaza and I, were the "regulars." There were also a few "irregulars," such as Paul.

Paul and his pretty sister Paula were twins. They had been born out of wedlock although their cantankerous father, a communist who paid little attention to conventional procedures, eventually consented to go through the motions of a formal wedding. However, after a while, he became disenchanted with his wedded state and his new familial duties. He soon started to disappear for weeks on end. It was left to their mother to try to eke out a living by working in a factory in Fulda. Every payday, she came to see my mother to work out a new revolving strategy for the repayment of the tremendous debts she owed our store. I am still at a loss to explain how the twins managed to develop into well adjusted adults.

The eastern part of the church plaza was our playground, an area about fifty by seventy feet, formed east and north by the ten-foot-high wall that slung from the manse to our store, and west and south by the northeastern recess of the tall, cross-shaped church building.

Whenever Dr. Winter stormed out of his manse to chase us, we ran away fast and moved our game to the main road. As soon as the danger had passed, our soccer game shifted back to the churchyard.

Since regular soccer balls were much too expensive, we would use any size ball, even a two inch ball. When our collective search failed to garner a ball at all, we would even play with a rock or a puck.

Our parents had strictly forbidden us to wear our "good" shoes when we were playing ball, and this became one of the few parental injunctions with which we complied. As a rule, we would spend the greater part of the afternoon playing ball. In later years, when I went to school in Fulda, my loving and incredibly patient mother used to wait up for me to serve me a late lunch at about 2 P.M. The moment I finished eating, I got up, changed my shoes, and ran down to play ball, thoughtlessly leaving my dear mother sitting there without the hoped-for report of the day's happenings in school, nor would I take care of my homework. Only many years later, too late, did I realize the anguish I must have caused her by not giving her at least a stripped-down version of the day's events in school.

One of the other "irregulars" in our soccer team was Walter Tölle, the younger of the two sons of Dr. Tölle, the village physician. He was somewhat overweight and his coordination was not such as to make him a good soccer player. He was much better as a bicyclist. Often, we would ride toward Schlüchtern, past the *Leide*, a beautiful pine forest, and race each other home.

The high windows of the baroque church were made of stained glass sections, depicting all kinds of religious motifs. Knowing that those stained windows did not come cheap, we were extremely careful to keep our ball, or its facsimile, close to the ground.

Unfortunately, our best intentions were sometimes thwarted in the heat of the action, and a well-intentioned shot might go astray, and shatter one of those precious stained glass panels. It happened only a few times, but each occasion was traumatic.

One time, one of my fellow players bungled and shot a three or four inch hole in a glass panel. While everybody else ran away in a different direction I, for reasons that have long since escaped me, stayed right there, my eyes riveted to that spot, knowing full well that Dr. Winter would presently flit through the gate that separated his manse and the church plaza, and demand an account.

Indeed, it took but a few seconds when the wooden gate flung open and Dr. Winter came flying through it. He was dressed in his black vestment which had flared open. It made him look like a giant blackbird with his wings spread wide. Out of reverence for him, I hesitate to say that he was "hellbent" to catch the culprit. He almost ran me over, his neighbor's son who was all of eight or nine years old, but he stopped in time and asked with a stern face whether I had done it. Humbly, but firmly, I replied in the negative. He then asked me to name the sinner and I said that I did not know who had done it. Of course, this was a little white lie. He kept looking straight at me just as I looked back at him and, suddenly, he burst out laughing like I had never seen him laugh. I began to laugh with him too and this was the moment from which sprang a long period of harmony between Dr. Winter and me.

Often, he would let me enter his private library and loan me a few books to read and would inquire about my folks' well-being. At no time would he try to convert me or make any untoward suggestion.

One of the books from his library that fascinated me especially, was a biographical history of the Tyrolean folk hero Andreas Hofer. A staunch Catholic and a zealous if somewhat anachronistic devotee of the moribund Hapsburg dynasty, he became the leader of the Tyroleans in their struggle for reunification with the Austrian Empire, after Napoleon Bonaparte had incorporated Tyrol in his own empire. For a long time he led a guerilla war against the French but, in the end, he was betrayed and captured, and Napoleon ordered him shot in the north Italian city of Mantua.

After a few years, we shifted our sport to the *Leide* where the village fathers had recently built a ballpark primarily for our senior team in the pine forest off the main road to Schlüchtern.

I still recall that on the day after my bar mitzvah, a Sunday, when I had been given one of a boy's most treasured gifts, a pair of soccer boots, and a regulation size soccer ball too, I ventured out to the *Leide* with some of my pals.

I was wearing that beautiful, new, tailor-made, three-piece, navy blue serge suit that was the pride of my bar mitzvah and the exquisite gold watch, my godfather Uncle Siegmund's vaunted gift, dangled on a gold chain from my vest pocket. I ignored my father's stern warning not to play ball in this suit.

Well, it was mid-July, and a hot and humid summer day it was, and within minutes of our game I was perspiring profusely. Very carefully I laid my jacket down right behind the goal cage and tucked my vest with that super-precious gold watch inside my jacket. When I checked back at half time, the watch was gone.

As far as my father was concerned, I resigned myself to one of those regular spankings, not so much for having my watch stolen, as if that was not bad enough, but for having disobeyed his order. But how in the world was I to break this heartbreaking bit of news to my

18

gentle Uncle Siegmund? I still remember the crestfallen disbelief in his face when I came right out with it. It was awful!

SIX
Coming To Terms

At the time when I was about thirteen, I began to wonder what my personal talents were and, like most kids of that age who had not already had their spirit broken by an unfortunate series of failures, or by some stupid reprimands or abuse by their peers or even their own parents or teachers, I spent a lot of thinking as to what I could do to further my talents as I perceived them, to do my own world-shaking deed, for was that not the ultimate goal of a human being's destiny on earth: shake the world, leave a mark!

One of the skills that came to mind was the electrical know-how that *Herr* Lotz had imparted to me. Another was the manual skill that I knew I possessed in fixing broken-down bicycles, for example. That included an understanding of the coaster brake mechanism, and the ability to repair it. I realized that particular feat required a certain degree of sophistication and I felt that I "had it."

This kind of consciousness and motivation, as everybody knows, is essential for generating the special effort needed to train yourself for the ultimate task of being as good as anybody else in at least one area of human endeavor. *Herr* Lotz proved to be my role model.

One day, as the result of such thinking, I built a suspension railroad along the entire length of our *Altane* (balcony). I took two bicycle coaster brakes and fastened their shafts to the two terminal piers of our balcony. Then I looped a light steel rope around the coaster brakes, wrapping the steel rope several times around one hub for greater friction, the one to be my "driver," while the other brake hub was to be my "idler," and fastened the loose ends tightly together. I laced both sides of the wire loop through a cigar box which I had carefully cleaned and painted inside and out and provided with square windows. Fastening my railroad carriage to one of the sides of the loop while letting the other side slip freely through it in the opposite direction, the steel cable became the suspension as well as the driving element whenever I rotated the drive coaster by means of a crank attached thereto. The driving cable also doubled up as one branch of the electrical circuit. The other wire that I needed to complete the circuit was stretched between the two terminal "stations" above the carriage. With the help of a transformer that could be plugged into a regular power outlet, I had a plentiful supply of low voltage electricity for the flashlight bulb that illuminated the inside of my single carriage train, and the green and red light bulbs inside the railroad signal light positioned about halfway along the route.

This must have been in the middle of summer, since it was the time cousin Irma was visiting us during her school vacation. When Irma first looked at my project she became so enthused she predicted that I would some day become a "famous" engineer. But Erwin's cousin Benjamin from New York who had come to visit us too during his own summer vacation, was notably jealous, and he tried hard to pick a fight with me. Before I realized it, he lunged at me and I was forced to beat him up. After that, he avoided me.

Another technical venture came a couple of years later. Uncle Nathan Katz and Tante Becka had their silver wedding in 1927 when I was twelve years old. Our family's gift to them was one of those newfangled radios. I had strict orders never to touch their radio, except for turning it on or off. In the following year, our parents celebrated their own silver wedding, and this time the Katzes presented them with a radio too but of a more advanced design. Although my parents and brothers Julius and Theo warned me not to fool around with it, I could not wait to lay my hands on it.

Since the store part of our large building had no attic and was therefore about ten feet lower than the residential section, it seemed logical to me to string our radio antenna from the projecting sidewall of the higher building to a pole that had to be fastened above the far end of our store building.

Just as my project was nearly finished and I was standing high on a ladder propped against the side of the store so I could tighten the loop of the antenna wire at the top of the pole, my father came up the street and caught sight of me. In my desperate plight, I quickly tightened the wire and climbed down the ladder where my father stood as a one-man reception committee. He started to spank me even before we both reached our house, in front of several curious onlookers.

However, my venture paid off, and we now had our very own orchestra, news service and weather forecasting system, right in our living room, much to the envy of our neighbors.

Before long, I found out that our radio could also be used as an amplifying system simply by plugging a loudspeaker into one of its spare outlets, in place of a microphone. That is how I set up "Radio Flieden." Inconspicuously, I strung bell wires from my bedroom to our store and connected them to a loudspeaker which I placed on a high shelf in the store. Some time later, I sent cousin Irma, who had been watching me, down to the store to hear my announcement: "Hello, hello, this is Radio Flieden." Uncle Nathan, too, heard it from his office and came flitting through the door. As soon as he realized what was going on, he climbed up to the high shelf, picked up the speaker and in great anger, like Moses with the tablets of the Ten Commandments before him, smashed the speaker to the stone floor, thus producing a premature end to my youthful entrepreneurship.

My Father

My father had a terrible time adjusting himself to the new world that came about in the aftermath of the First World War, a world that became increasingly unglued. He had been brought up in the simple and narrow confines of a Jewish peasant family in a Hessian village which had largely remained untouched by the major developments of the past century. Compared to his birthplace, Oberaula, even the village of Flieden seemed centuries ahead.

There is an interesting documentation in the *Jewish Encyclopedia* as to my paternal forefathers' history. It seems to be well established that they were among the people forced to leave Spain in that fateful year of 1492. They fled to the Netherlands where the latent rebellion against the hated Spanish rule had produced a climate of compassion for all victims of that rule.

However, when King Charles V of Spain, who himself was Dutch-born, retired to a monastery in 1556 and turned his rule over to his straight-laced son Philip, the relative benevolence with which the Spanish kings had treated the Netherlands began to turn to unremitting intransigence, particularly after the arrival of the uncompromising and hateful Duke of Alba, and the Dutch people began to organize for their ultimate rebellion. In the meantime, the Jews who had fled there from Spain, feared for the full-scale introduction of the murderous Inquisition in Holland, and were happy to receive an invitation from the reform-minded Duke of Mansbach in Hesse to settle there.

It was not at all strange that, three hundred years later, my father was born in a village just a few miles from that Duchy. Alas, by then its glory had ended and the territory, ravaged by centuries of warfare that accompanied the demise of the feudal system in most of Germany, had sunk into a cultural netherworld.

Paradoxically, one of the few nice things that may be said about the "Iron Chancellor" Bismarck, was that his unification of Germany provided the deathknell to feudalism, and brought a fairly uniform educational system to the provinces of the Reich.

As a result, my father's education was not unlike the one that *Herr* Freudenberger dispensed. However, my father was imbued with an extra ambition, and that was to study the Hebrew language, and in that he was rather successful. Every Saturday afternoon he would gather a group of youngsters around him, in addition to his own children for whom participation was, of course, mandatory, and teach us one chapter or another of that ubiquitous everyday guide for orthodox Jews, the *Shulchan Aruch.*

Besides his knowledge of Hebrew, my father was quite an expert in geography and history, all self-taught. By listening to his discussing all kinds of subjects with my brother Theo, I think a lot of knowledge rubbed off on me and that undoubtedly made things a lot easier later on in high school.

When our family settled in 1929 in Fulda, a modern town of over thirty thousand people and a district capital, he would still get up every weekday morning at the crack of dawn, put his phylacteries in a pouch made of royal blue velvet and, rain or shine, walk to the synagogue to say his morning prayers as part of the minyan, which is synonymous with a minimum number of ten males over thirteen years old needed to validate the prayer service.

With all that, my father was a real autocrat and the least disagreement with his views by anybody was enough to arouse his spleen, sometimes to the point of physical abuse. Since my brother Theo was potentially his foremost competitor, it was also he who

23

bore the brunt of his ire and, frequently, Theo's black and blue eyes, or even a broken tooth, would attest to my father's temper.

It seems that the more my father had to confront new, untried experiences, the more he retreated into the protective shell of orthodoxy, and the more stubbornly he tried to shape the world around him, first of all his family, in his own, orthodox image.

There was hardly anybody in the village, particularly among the young people, who cared to cross his path, and for all his eminent knowledge, he was more feared than respected. To top it all, he came home from the war with a bad case of malaria and, periodically, as is wont with that dreaded disease, he would suffer relapses that were as bad as the original attack had been. On the whole, he surely made life a lot more difficult for a great many people than his religious mandate seemed to warrant.

At the same time, going through a losing war, winding up with a ravaging case of malaria, living through the Great Inflation and the Great Depression as a businessman and head of household and, finally, as a good veteran soldier of the German Imperial Army who treasured his Iron Cross, witnessing the growing inroads of Nazism, all that was enough to devastate anybody's sense of balance.

It is never easy for parents to understand the generation gap that seems to separate them from their children. This difficulty is compounded whenever the parents have been raised in a society where conventional values are hardly ever questioned, because "things were good enough for my parents; they are good enough for me, and should be good enough for you," and where "loyalty and duty" often have become rationales and laws unto themselves, while the children grow up in a new atmosphere where most or all of those values are constantly scrutinized and routinely questioned at every critical juncture.

I suppose the simplest way to characterize my father would be to describe him as a man with a lot of inner contradiction and to the extent to which he was conscious of them, with a sincere desire to resolve them. He was convinced that he was a true German patriot. He took great pride in his Gothic calligraphy. Although he became rather obese after his return from the war, he kept his posture as straight as though he had swallowed a Prussian ramrod. He would recite all kinds of patriotic poetry whenever the occasion arose. Once, on Armistice Day, 1924, I watched my father standing on the pedestal of the Village War Memorial in front of a couple of hundred veterans from the First World War. He was holding forth about the greatness of loving one's country. He concluded his speech with the famous rallying cry from Schiller's *William Tell,* "Join in with the fatherland, the dear one...", which words earned him thunderous applause from the crowd. I stood in the corner watching. I felt embarrassed though I did not know why.

His self-image was that of a German, but of the Jewish faith, both terms bearing strangely similar, orthodox connotations. He decided to follow the practice then prevailing among orthodox Jews in Germany of selecting non-Jewish first names for his children. In this manner, my older brother was given the name Julius, my second brother was Theodore, or Theo, for short. My sister's name was Elli, and I, the late arrival, became, horror of horrors, Berthold.

SEVEN
Triads

Nowadays, children are no longer considered a separate human species distinct from grown-ups or even adolescents. Child psychologists and modern parents are now in agreement that the younger segment of human beings, from an early age on, is pretty much endowed with all the basic physiological, psychological, even social attributes of the adults, albeit to a lesser degree. Conversely, they seem to suffer fewer of the often inexplicable aberration in which adults get themselves embroiled.

As a small child I too was considered distinctly different from the adults who comprised my environment, and I was considered so at least until I became bar mitzvah. For that reason, I was privy to many conversations that my elders conducted in my presence assuming that I was unable to understand them, much as people have no inhibition conversing about the most intimate subjects in the presence of cats and dogs, or canaries.

In this manner, I gained knowledge of a great many secrets that came through the grapevine, though the moral climate of the time precluded my sharing those secrets with anyone. It was only natural that my phantasies often went wild with speculation, for example, as to the origin of some new baby that often represented the topics of those stories. Some babies were born without the benefit of their parents' holy matrimony. Or who was whose wet nurse; why did not the natural mother nurse her own child? On another level, my father would discuss politics with his contemporaries in my presence and often the politician under discussion was found to be corrupt. Since everybody in our culture was supposed to rise and fall with the three-cornered classical fountainhead of "Goodness, Truth and Beauty," those tidbits sent out unmistakable signals of skepticism to a very alert youngster.

It was at that time that a practical bit of human psychology and wisdom that my mother had evolved came to my rescue.

It had always been incomprehensible to us children and to her friends and even her relatives, how well my mother "handled" our temperamental father. When she was questioned about it, she would simply say that she would never react to his ravings and rantings until he had calmed down, and then she could usually make him see things her way. This must have been true, for I do not remember any time that the two had a violent argument. She was a veritable saint!

An even more important bit of her philosophy that she shared freely with everybody, was her habit of dividing people into three categories: The good ones, the bad ones, and the hard to tell.

However, in human terms, this mathematically unassailable division was subject to certain modifications. It was obvious, she told us, that not all good people were good all the time, nor all bad people were bad all the time. Those that were either all good or all bad were usually only found in literature.

Needless to say that my mother tried to keep the people she had designated as bad, or even the uncertain group, at arm's length, out of harm's way. Just the same, it was always puzzling to us how she succeeded at having so many friends with whom she had an abiding relationship of mutual trust, not only in Flieden but also throughout that vast hinterland of ours where many people had also been long-time patrons of our store. Even in her later years, she corresponded regularly with some of her childhood friends.

Naturally, there were exemplifications of the reverse part of her psychology too in our everyday lives. For example, every Sunday when mass was over and half the churchgoers would spill into our store to do their weekly shopping, we youngsters were told to watch out for certain individuals who had been known in the past to steal merchandise during those hectic store hours.

Even at my tender age, it did not take long until my mother's approach to life and people rubbed off on me and became a part of my own instinct and behavior baggage. Later on, when things got rough and tough for us, my mother's psychological legacy came in very handy. It helped me cope with many seemingly insuperable adversities and preserve my sanity. The truth is that I soon became adept in the art of assessing people as to what category he or she belonged from the very moment I laid eyes on them. Was he a "good" one, a "bad" one, or an "I don't know" one? Later, in the Nazi years, this talent provided me with a priceless edge in many critical encounters.

Yet, after a while, it occurred to me that during periods of great stresses and frustrations, whole layers of people in those three basic categories undergo shifts in their former positions, almost always toward the bad side. The badies themselves get more obnoxious, and their numbers are reinforced by those that formerly belonged to the middle group. In a narrow sense, history could be construed as a record of those shifts, sometimes proceeding in an evolutionary fashion and, at other times, when the people at the top are too rigid to make allowances for the people's changed feelings, producing a veritable blowout, a revolution.

However, when stresses become so intolerable that they get completely out of control, there seems to be a slide into the "Nietzsche Phenomenon," and whole masses of people follow some "inner lead," at great variance to and often in total opposition to their very own interests. History has many examples where the beginning of a war, or a "great victory" is, as a rule, greeted by the most hysterical, often completely unwarranted, approval of a large segment of the population.

In the case of Nazi Germany, it soon became clear that Goebbels' propaganda machine cooked up such a never-ending sequence of exciting events that many people were left in a state of addled confusion and their normal sense of righteousness became crippled. This outbreak of collective insanity may have been a means of self-preservation, no matter how dubious.

Naturally, there were times when my own categorizations proved rash and wrong. Once, for example, during a Zionist youth conference in Berlin I was walking with my pals in a street where some scaffolding extended halfway across the sidewalk. I noticed a man approaching the scaffold. He wore dark glasses and carried a cane to poke his way along. Just as I was making a mental note designating him as a "faker," he collided with the edge of the scaffold and hurt himself. This gave me a severe jolt the memory of which has lasted up to this day. I vowed never again to prejudge people before I had gotten to know them better, a formula that was sometimes hard and sometimes impossible to follow.

Little wonder that, at times, our judgment went haywire, particularly when it is considered that never since the Reign of Terror during the French Revolution, there existed such a widespread, wholly pervasive, wholly irrational, wholly impersonal fear of one's life that the Nazi propaganda machine had set in motion.

Terror stalked the streets. It permeated the workplace, the office and the home. It existed, unrelentingly, twenty-four hours of the day. There was no way that it could ever escape anybody's consciousness.

This was true for everybody from the very onset of the Nazi regime. But for Jewish people, the enactment of the "Nüremberg Laws" in September 1935, made everything perfectly "legal." It was almost miraculous that this total deprivation of all civil rights did not lead to the instant extermination of the Jewish people even then, five years before its final consummation, remembering that the call of "The Night of the Long Knives" had long been a rallying cry of the right-wing deviates. The only tempering that can be invoked under the circumstances, was the inherent decency of a great many Germans, although that decency was never allowed to be verbalized in public, or to have a visible surface, but it was perceived as a powerful force, nevertheless, by the Nazi brutes.

Although the Nazi propaganda machine tried hard to belittle the significance or even denied the existence of this moral force and never permitted it to be visible, or articulated, it cannot and must not ever be questioned that this very real resistance was the only counterpoise to Hitler's craven wishes being carried out instantly. It was the only counterweight in existence. As it happened, it took Goebbels years of intimidation, cajolery and threats to bulldoze most everybody to accept the preordained inevitability.

The individual's task was to conduct himself well below the threshold of visibility so as not to provide the Nazis with a more plausible rationalization for "action."

In the end, as the befuddlement and the paranoia of the German people by the Nazi-controlled media took on greater and greater proportions and everybody was tossed about in the maelstrom of ethical chaos, it became altogether impossible to determine who was friend or foe, and these former characterizations lost their usefulness.

Settling Down

I was about ten years old when I mustered my first attempt to develop a philosophy of life. In retrospect, it seemed a crude attempt, but at the time I felt that I was old enough.

The first thing I did, in the stillness of my bedroom, was to check out the existence of God. I started by saying a prayer, one of the everyday prayers in the liturgy and waited for some divine response. Since there was no reaction of any kind, I decided that religion was not for me and that was that. At the same time, I allowed that some of the basic tenets like the Ten Commandments, or Hillel's and Jesus' advocacy of love for one's neighbor, were eminently worthwhile principles to emulate. Much later, I realized that my simplistic approach was not really all that stupid. After all, two fellows in ancient Alexandria, Philo and Plotin, spent a lifetime trying to reconcile religion and morality.

I believe that the lack of any divine response or even recognition absolved me forever from that kind of guilt feelings from which so many "sinners" seem to suffer, and saved me from any subconscious desire as well to inflict punishment upon myself to atone for my "sins," or atone for my father's sins whatever they were.

It was many years later that I realized that a lot of people use religion as a crutch to rationalize their guilt feelings, and do all kinds of penance to satisfy their masochism, a sort of danse macabre, carried out prematurely in their own lifetime, even long before they would, by dint of the scriptural mandate, wind up in hell or Hades. They evolve the "alter ego" of a schizophrenic type of duality to sustain their immaculate conduct and thereby absolve themselves from the acrimonious errors of their real self regardless of merit. Others try to act out their guilt complex, impersonating their own, warped self-image, and thus become "bad" people. We often overlook the social origin of these feelings of inadequacy and guilt in people who blame themselves for their failures in the labor market or business life as though their lack of success was wholly or even partly due to their personal shortcomings. I am thinking here of sincere people, not of those consummate politicians who use religious or moral tenets consciously and deliberately for their own dirty ends.

When I looked around myself, I realized that I was the youngest person in the two families forming the inner circle of my existence.

My own family, the Wallachs, had three sons and a daughter, Julius, Theo, Elli and myself, in that order, the Katzes had five children, Lina, Rudi, Bella, Walter and Erwin.

We had maids who, usually after a few years, would leave us as soon as they had found a husband. They were then replaced by unattached ones. There were many young girls eager to serve in a home as renowned as ours. The maids in our household were well thought of and routinely garnered the most eligible bachelors in the village. Because of her vast circle of friends, my mother had a virtually inexhaustible number of candidates for those jobs on hand and was glad to pass some on to our relatives and friends.

Occasionally, my mother's selection on the basis of her three moral categories misfired, and several times, one or another of the young ladies that she had selected for our friends would either become pregnant or would steal from her employers. Within the framework of my mother's ethical terminology, these maids fell short of expectations. When some of these stories came to my father's attention, he laid down the law to my mother that she must stop "doing good," otherwise there would be no end of trouble. Grudgingly, my mother complied.

Of course, there were some outright jewels among our maids with whom we children formed attachments that lasted forever, that even survived fascism's ugly assault upon the human race. How could I ever forget the visit Carol and I paid to Bertha Heil, Isidor's sister, when we came back to Flieden for the first time after the war! Bertha was on her deathbed, and she was unable to speak, except to groan "Jesus, Maria, mother of God!"

She wanted to know all about my family. When I came to report tearfully about my sister Elli having perished somewhere in a forest near Riga, Bertha went into convulsions, and everybody in the room, all the twenty people that had come with us, including her two sons and her two daughters, feared that she would not survive another moment. Actually, she lingered on a few more weeks.

She came from an exceptional family and, as I was to learn much later, was herself the progenitress of an exceptional family.

We had a whole string of "good" maids. They would get up early in the morning, winter and summer, make fires and boil coffee, set the breakfast table for the standard menu: corn bread that was baked in one of the three village ovens and for which my father had purchased flour from some local farmers, and butter which was of course homemade, too. Except for the fall, after the fruit was harvested and preserved, jam was hardly ever served at the table.

Lunch was mostly the same as breakfast, a cup of coffee, and a piece of bread and butter. Supper was our main meal. Invariably, it consisted of a piece of meat, mostly beef, a thick gravy and potatoes. In summer, we also had vegetables from our two gardens. There were Brussels sprouts, spinach, cauliflower, carrots, peas, beans, white and red cabbage, and a delectable Boston lettuce.

Saturday nights, we usually had herring with boiled potatoes and sour cream. On the whole, our diet left much to be desired in terms of present days' standards of nutrition.

Except for herring, fish was served only during the holidays. Just before the Hanukkah week, our kosher butcher would come to our house and convert a quarter of a freshly slaughtered steer into delicious sausages with plenty of salt and pepper. They would then get smoked in some local smokehouse and for months served as our standard sandwich food. The longer these sausages would be hanging in the pantry, the harder and saltier they would get, and the more they became a hazard to one's teeth. But they were sooo delicious!

Anybody describing our childhood pleasures without referring to these sausages would commit an unforgivable sin. That night we were allowed to stay up longer and we were treated to a large piece of a freshly boiled sausage with a slice of corn bread.

Besides the tasks of cooking, our maids also had to take care of cleaning the house once a week, to wash the laundry and hang it up for drying. When we acquired a dog and a cat, it was our maid's duty to feed them, keep a dish filled with water, and protect them from abuse that we children might try to inflict on them.

Our dog, in particular, was rather attractive. At a shoulder height of about eighteen inches, his body was covered with short black hair, his legs were all gold. Interestingly, he had a large white cross of hair on his chest. When my brother Julius brought him home he was barely five weeks old. Hence, we knew his true mother, but his paternal origin remained forever unknown. Despite his lack of pedigree, he was a remarkable canine. He was good as a watchdog, and learned to perform some of the tricks of a circus dog, such as shaking hands, or paws, walking through the room on his hind legs, and jumping through a ring. Whenever he considered us children menaced by anybody he would defend us fiercely. When we sometimes had an intra-family spat with hints of a physical resolution, he would display a remarkable sense of "pecking order" invariably protecting the weakest. Brother Julius insisted that he even knew some Hebrew. To prove it, he would offer him a slice of sausage and say "akol!" (eat!). This particular feat would always produce a hilarious outburst by the onlookers.

Because the Germans still hated the British much more than the "decadent" French on account of their proverbial endurance in battle which, in their eyes, had made Germany ultimately lose the war, our dog was called "Tommy" by consensus. Yet his loyalty to us was without flaw. When Tommy was about eight years old, he was run over by an automobile, and died after three days of lingering. During that time, I sat down with him on the kitchen floor and observing the unspeakable sadness in his eyes, I was sure he knew that he was going to die. After he was dead, about a dozen of my pals gathered, put his body in a wooden box, and gave him a dignified burial emulating Dr. Winter's human precedents.

Another of the weekly chores for our maids was the preparation for the baths every Thursday evening. At that time, hot water systems were hardly known, even coal-heated boilers had not yet come into use. So every Thursday night, two huge tinned steel kettles were filled with cold water from the faucet and then heated up on our oven. We then took turns bathing in an oval tub which at other times also served as laundry.

Naturally, as the youngest, I came first. As I was whisked away to my bed in the back room, it was my sister Elly's turn, and she took her bath in the same water that I had used. That was the rule in our house: Two people for one tub full of water.

Next came my two brothers, Julius and Theo, who also had to put up with one tub of water between them. Then came our various maids, employees, Tante Emmy and whoever was a visitor.

My cousin Irma spent all her summer vacations with us in Flieden, and came to be considered by us as another sister. She was a couple of years older than I was and at that age, her breasts had already developed to an intriguing degree. I decided to try to get a closer look when she was going to have her weekly bath. It so happened that, in the past, somebody had drilled a hole in the wooden wall that separated my bedroom from the pantry, and the pantry door into the kitchen where the bathing took place, was usually wide open, and that is how I hoped to satisfy my curiosity as to what the female anatomy looked like.

It all worked out very well and, for the first time in my life, I got a clear picture of what had been withheld from me in this post-Victorian atmosphere of ours for so long. At my cousin's tender age of about thirteen, she was already quite pretty and well proportioned, and I felt good about knowing her a lot better now.

History Intrudes

In the fourth year of our elementary school, cousin Erwin and I were given French lessons in preparation of attending the *Oberrealschule* in Fulda, the following year. Our parents hoped that with French tutoring, we would be allowed to jump the *Sexta*, (first grade) and start in the *Quinta* (second grade).

This hope came true. One sunny, but chilly morning in April of 1926, my mother Recha and Erwin's mother, Aunt Becka, took us on an electric train to Fulda to take our second-year entrance exams. Thanks to *Herr* Freudenberger's teaching we had no problem passing. Within a week, we had become members of the *Quinta* class, section "B" with Dr. Johann Stöhr as the principal teacher, a role which he kept, year after year, during our entire stay in that school.

Erwin and I had also become quasi-permanent fixtures in the electric commuter train in the morning and the express train in the afternoon. We were easily recognized by our green school caps with their silver ribbons and our leather briefcases that had replaced the traditional rucksacks of our elementary school days.

Jumping the *Sexta* produced a few unexpected results. For one thing, it made me the youngest in the class and that bloated my self-image far beyond its legitimate entitlement.

Before long, my cousin Erwin assumed the role of my shammash. He collected the material for our homework. He came to my house every morning to make sure that we would not miss our train and be late for class. He would check whether I had all the right books, my homework, even my luncheon for that day in my leathercase.

Since Erwin grew up in a family which was in almost all respects similar to my own, I have often wondered why we developed so differently. Maybe it can be blamed on our different "genes."

Interesting as all these incidents that occurred in the narrow realm of our personal lives may have been, they contributed little to the dramatic events that filled the history of our time. Conversely, it was precisely those historic events that occurred in the global macrocosm that produced a far more lasting effect on us. In fact, those events shook our own little world to its very foundation and sent shock waves throughout the universe that have not entirely subsided unto this day. They established themselves, quite rudely, as the major determinants of our future.

It soon became clear to everybody that the war was not the only thing that had come to an end in Germany. The imperial Kaiser Reich that the "Iron Chancellor" Bismarck had built up so carefully, was in shambles too. Not much of that pseudo-patriotic battle cry "For God, Kaiser and Fatherland" had withstood the millions of bullets, shells and grenades, the deaths, the wounds and destruction of four years of bloody trench warfare.

Unemployment became endemic. When the unemployment benefits ran out, they were superseded by the demeaning and hateful welfare system. One cannot imagine the sense of frustration that befell the once proud German worker as he was forced to his knees.

This pervasive unemployment produced a vast reservoir of available labor and that in turn created a severe depression of wages. Before long, Uncle Nathan, who, if you remember, was our bookkeeper and accountant, tried vainly to cope with two huge ledgers filled with the names of thousands of lifelong customers who owed us unreal amounts of money. To use a more modern term, our cashflow had virtually ceased to exist. All of a sudden, life itself seemed to have lost its luster.

EIGHT
High School

Our high school class, *Quinta* B, had thirty-two students. In the beginning there were twelve Catholics, twelve Protestants, and eight Jewish students. The inevitable formation of cliques, however, did not occur along religious lines.

To be sure, the top students, being boosted at every opportunity by our principal teacher, Dr. Stöhr, formed one distinct group. Another group, partly overlapping the former, were the sportsmen, particularly the members of the school's soccer team. A third group consisted of those students that had failed the previous grade and had been left behind from the previous *Quinta*, and were, therefore, one or even two years older than we were.

Despite their academic shortcomings, however, they were generally considered street-wise. For example, when I first learned about sex at the relatively "ripe old age" of my early teens, having been "protected" by my saintly mother for so long, I always fancied that they had been into it for quite a while.

As could be expected, one group consisted of the rich kids, but in our class, they also happened to be the non-achievers and they never came into great prominence. For one thing, they routinely visited the better students to copy their homework.

Our teachers represented a fair cross-section of the population. We addressed them by their names, as *Herr* So-and-So, unless they had a Ph.D., or had attained the title of professor. In this provincial town, many of our teachers had acquired a nickname, and a reputation that went with it, usually unflattering. Although I was always very conscious of their sobriquets, I was careful never to use them, lest somebody might squeal on me.

It was easy to classify all the students as "good" people. We did not have one single bully in our class. On the other hand, among our teachers there were some that I considered doubtful.

One of the most unforgettable, if not disagreeable, characters of that time was our art teacher. His task was to instruct us in drawing and painting as well as in appreciation of the arts and music. It soon became apparent that he suffered from a sort of mental depression which the collective wisdom of this twelve to thirteen year old class attributed to shell shock suffered in World War I.

He would deliver his lessons in a most unendurably boring manner, bereft of any worthwhile content. Soon the entire class was transformed into a number of conversation groups and, for a while, he did not seem to notice. Suddenly, like a bolt out of the blue, he would jump up and rap his big stick on the table and fall into a hysterical tirade of tremendous decibels as to our lack of appreciation and gratitude to him, a world war veteran, who had laid his life on the line to allow us unworthy creatures to live.

Once, he not only hit the nearest table but also the nearest student, and overwhelmed by his own outrage, broke into uncontrolled sobbing. This time he had clearly gone too far. We formed a delegation and reported this incident and others preceding it to the school principal and that is how we got a new and more tolerable teacher of the arts, *Herr* Maler.

Herr Maler was a devotee of the classical school of music and on occasion conducted the local, third-rate symphony orchestra in Fulda. With some of us, his love of Haydn, Mozart, Beethoven and Schubert was just fine. He surely qualified as one of my mother's good people. He loved not just the classic composers, he loved all mankind. He loved his students far beyond a teacher's call of duty.

While listening one day with great intensity to *Herr* Maler's piano playing, as he led a musical parade of long past eras in front of us, the thought flashed through my mind that musical "periods" and "styles" are more than just passing fads and fancies to which the contemporary crop of composers, painters, architects, or writers happens to subscribe. This was the moment when I felt certain that I had made a tremendous discovery which I wanted to test in the near future.

All of a sudden it became clear to me that the true greatness of an artist cannot only be measured by his superior expression of the moods, feelings, fears and aspirations of his times, but must be evaluated by the degree of his commitment to a resolution of these problems with their multi-sided aspects. Whoever reads with an open mind the masterful story of Heinrich von Kleist's *Michael Kohlhaas*, for example, is bound to recognize the portrait of a human being within his society whose own personal fight against injustice burgeons into a universal, encompassing and ultimately devouring crusade against tyranny in all its manifestations.

Who can deny that perhaps the greatest star of the art universe, Ludwig von Beethoven, in total consciousness of his act, refused to kowtow to the Emperor Napoleon as soon as he recognized that Napoleon had become a traitor to the very ideas of the French Revolution to which he had originally dedicated his ambitions?

How Beethoven then refused to write any meaningful composition for a full decade sensing with great bitterness the reactionary nature of the very forces that had brought Napoleon down and had, in his stead, instituted a regime of censorship, police spittles, and anti-people policies. It took years of soul-searching until he felt certain that there must be inherent values in life itself in the face of all adversities, and he brought forth the miracle of the *Ninth Symphony*, a paean of life and brotherhood arising from the ashes of various unacceptable philosophies, lifestyles and cultures.

Alas, unlike Beethoven, the great writers and composers of the romantic period who grew up in the era of regimentation and repression, were not possessed of the same stamina. Individually and as a group, they were unable to bridge the gap between their idealistic aspirations and dreams, and the brutal reality of their everyday life. They either fell into the protecting veil of insanity, like Schuhmann, Hölderlin, Platen, and Lenau, or committed suicide, like Kleist. Paradoxically, Keats, Shelley, Novalis, Schubert and Chopin were perhaps the most fortunate of all the Romantics in that fate extinguished their blazoning candle at a tragically young age.

Of course, the art of painting did not suffer as much from the rigors of an oppressive regime. It was relatively easy and not as unsettling for the painters of this period to turn to the noncommittal world of landscapings and portraiture. No censorship there!

Luckily, in our own little world, the composers, both classical and romantic, were *Herr* Maler's exclusive preoccupation.

I still remember him sitting at the piano with his bald head that looked like a flesh colored soccer ball and, with heart and soul, hammer out the first portentous chords of Beethoven's *Fifth Symphony* that later became the symbol of the English people's indomitable spirit of resistance to the Nazis. Before long, his lessons turned into a dialogue between *Herr* Maler and some of us.

We graduated in 1934, the second year of the Nazi regime. No other teacher had the courage of his convictions to give anyone of us four Jewish graduates any but a passing mark, but *Herr* Maler insisted that in art appreciation I receive an "A."

To be sure, no matter what our graduating report card would have said, even if we had had all As, by the spring of 1934, it had become impossible for a Jewish graduate to enter a university, one whole year before the Nuremberg Laws made the exclusion "legal." When, on a chilly April morning, Dr. Stöhr asked each student what professional choice he should enter on the graduation certificate, I cried out defiantly "mechanic" which he, mercifully, changed to "pursuit of a technical profession."

It was but a short week later, when the four of us were summoned before the high school principal, Dr. Lauwartz, presumably to receive our graduating papers and at the same time listen to an insincere sermon of good wishes for our future. In our defiance we had already divided up the collective piece of mind that each of us was to give him. However, our tainted opinion about him changed as soon as he began to talk to us, and we had to conclude that it was he who had managed to persuade the local Nazi bigwigs to let us graduate at all, and for that, he had gotten himself into hot water with the Nazis.

Alas, when he handed us our graduating certificates signed by him and Dr. Stöhr, we discovered sadly that, but for *Herr* Maler's mark, all we had received were Cs, an obvious compromise between Dr. Lauwartz and the Nazi mayor. Incidentally, it was this same mayor who, during the stiff graduating ceremony, gave the valedictory, a role that, according to many of Dr. Stöhr erstwhile announcements, had originally been assigned to me.

NINE
The Depression

History, it is true, proceeds in giant steps and in its wild path is no respecter of individuals or people. However, when the chronicler wishes to give a true account, he is often torn between carrying one particular story to the bitter end and picking up the thread of another, concurrent, story later on or, as an alternative method, move across the pages with all his stories simultaneously. His strategy depends somewhat on his estimate of the reader's intelligence, memory and often, patience.

The dramatist, on the other hand, can afford to use the broad advance style of several of his armies, so to speak, letting the spotlight shine on this main event of the moment or on that, simply because the observer has one extra sense to help him sort things out, his eyes. Hence, we ask the reader to proceed in full awareness of these difficult alternatives for the writer.

For example, in the previous chapter we have peeked ahead to the middle thirties, yet we are actually still very much in the time frame of the mid-twenties, specifically 1926, 1927 and 1928.

Those were the years that followed the Great Inflation, and they tended to restore a sense of stability, if not outright prosperity, to Germany and the entire Western world. In the rose-shaded eyes of the European and American middle classes, it was hoped that the seven lean years had, at long last, given way to seven fat years.

In retrospect, this turned out to be a case of self-deception. It is true that the western world was blessed with five years of generally increasing wages and buying power, but the resulting expansion and updating of the manufacturers' production facilities, based on the euphoric hope that, from now on, the economy would have a smooth road ahead, came to a cropper just a few years hence.

In the firm of Isaiah Katz, too, things began to look up at first during that period, and even my father, who had carried on as a veritable prophet of doom, began to make plans for the future. For many years already, our store, for all practical purposes, consisted of a textile section, supervised by my father with the assistance of my two brothers Julius and Theo and my sister Elli, and everything else under the jurisdiction of my uncle Nathan Katz, assisted by two of his five children, my cousins Bella and Walter. Their older sister, Lina, and their brother, Rudi, were both hard of hearing. Rudi was relegated to fixing bicycles and other equipment. He also took care of shipping and receiving. My cousin Erwin and I, of course, were still attending high school.

However, when my father and my brother Theo, who was gifted with an excellent business sense, analyzed the relative share of sales and profits, they found that the bulk of the business was carried by the Wallachs, and that the Katz family brought little profit to the store. The outcome of that analysis was a heart-rending decision to dissociate from the Katz family, and set up shop in Fulda. To buy us out, Uncle Nathan Katz turned to his American brothers-in-law, Jacob and Dave Neuhaus, and borrowed the necessary money. Our move to Fulda also brought an end to my commuting from Flieden that I had done for four years in the company of my cousin Erwin to attend the *Oberrealschule*. Now, it was a five-minute walk.

The beginning of our family's new venture in Fulda in the summer of 1929, seemed to augur well for a successful future. We offered a diversified line of textiles, popular with our old customers from Flieden and its hinterland, as well as the new ones from Fulda and environs. Alas, the newly generated optimism, shared this time even by our father, did not last. Just as we were looking forward to a great Christmas season, there took place, in the United States at first, the start of the Great Depression, exploding with the New York Stock Market crash of "Black Thursday," October 24, 1929. Within the space of just a few months, the rate of unemployment in Germany, still high from the Great Inflation, more than tripled. It was a real epidemic; words alone cannot describe it adequately.

Prior to the Great Depression, Germany, in its eagerness to rebuild its industry even beyond its pre-war glory, had become the largest debtor of the United States. Because of the great promise of the

German economic resurrection, its bonds were eagerly bought up by profit-hungry American investors.

However, disaster lurked just around the corner. To be sure, during the first ten months of 1929 the New York stock market did indeed bounce up amid a wave of euphoric craze and all available money went into stocks. Many European bonds were called to have more investment money available and the stock market reached an all-time high. Few investors had any inkling that all that hurrah was without a solid foundation and that the tremendous amount of credit was like a huge sand castle, ready to collapse.

The collapse came with a vengeance. Starting with Black Thursday, it took no more than three weeks for the average stock to come down to half its previous value, many stocks disappearing altogether. The panic of the New York stock market and the ensuing frenzy of the traders to retrieve a modicum of their former wealth, brought about bank runs and distress sales of bonds and other monetary instruments at home and an even more frantic withdrawal from the European money and investment market which, in turn, caused the collapse of countless banks and credit institutions there.

Virtually millions saw their life savings melt away, sometimes within the space of just a few days and the failure of small and medium businesses, banks and farms became rampant. While the failure of such important sectors of the economy was by itself catastrophic, the effect on employment was even more disastrous. Within a few months of the Depression, unemployment in the United States, where no social security at all existed, reached beyond the 30 percent mark. Yet in Germany the situation was worse.

From the purchase of raw materials, to production, to distribution, to consumption, to housing and employment, none of the elements of the supply and demand relationship seemed to work anymore.

However, while the American people were political "Babes in the Woods," the German people had emerged from the aftermath of the lost war and the great Inflation with a high degree of political consciousness, combined with a dangerous sense of frustration.

All of a sudden, the optimism of the recent past gave way to an all-pervasive sense of despair. From one day to the next, people literally had to spend every waking minute of their day with the task of obtaining the bare necessities of their and their family's life. To many millions, the quality and style of life itself had come down to that of animals of the wild.

It was not long before the new social and economic instability created an alarming polarization between the political right and left. The Communist party, whose attempted take over at the end of the war had been beaten back by the Social-Democratic government of the Weimar Republic, some used the word "betrayed," was growing again and soon surpassed the Social Democrats.

However, it was the National Socialist German Workers' Party (Nazis, for short) who were most successful in taking advantage of the German misery. The party name itself was a clever, if not confusing mix of terms misappropriated from several reputable ideologies. The Nazis were making heavy inroads into the fast-fading middle class, the impoverished peasantry, and that segment of the German working class which blamed the Social Democrats for having betrayed them.

Finally, there were the lumpen, the rootless dregs of society, many of whom became the bloody butchers of the Holocaust. No doubt, they were the "badies," devoid of any solid viewpoint whatsoever.

The intelligent observer of the political scene was forced to the conclusion that, in time of severe crisis, many people develop an urge to throw themselves at the mercy of their worst enemies. They follow a morbid desire to kiss the boot that kicks them in the rear, a modern replay of the flagellants. Nietzsche once said while insanity seemed to be rare among individuals, when it came to groups of people it was the rule rather than the exception.

It is well-nigh impossible in this latter-day flashback to recollect the exact motives that prompted us, six students in our class, in the year 1930, to get together for the exalted purpose of studying philosophy. Undoubtedly, there was the natural curiosity of the adolescent as to what holds the world together, where we come from, and where we are going. Beyond that, moreover, there existed a powerful need to build a wall against the onslaught of the many raging and confusing ideological storms that were sweeping all around us with ever-increasing fury.

Our intellectual enterprise started out in a stiff fashion and, for a while, we had very mixed feelings about it. But soon our presumptuous initiative turned into a welcome medium for relief in the sense that "misery loves company." To use another metaphor, it became a well-disciplined, mental free-for-all.

Each period of history seems to generate its own cultural parameters as a natural reflection of the specific concerns of the contemporaries and the impact upon them. Everybody who is resolved to live his or her own life in optimal consciousness and control, evolves a desire to break through the masquerade that the particular "establishment" tries at all times to deploy on the people. That may be the reason why in times of oppression, the cry of freedom becomes ever stronger, in times of war, peace becomes the people's priority, and in times of confusion, new philosophies and new religions are born, or reborn.

This consideration also explains that it was not our arrogance as semiliterates in the field of philosophy, but a natural reaction on our part that helped us in our decision to make short shrift of all the philosophers of the past who labored hard to prove in one form or another that the "idea" is the primary and perfect aspect of all things and the real thing is but an imperfect representation and reflection of that idea. To us, however, the question of what came first, the chicken or the egg, bore no particular relevance compared to the very real choices of socialism, democracy or fascism.

We found that no matter from what culture those idealistic philosophers sprang, whether they were pagan such as Plato, or religious like St. Augustine, somehow, they always wound up with concepts that promised salvation only to a small fraction of mankind, namely the conformists, the pious, the bigots and occasionally, toadies while the major part of humanity was condemned to a status of social and spiritual slavery or even hell. In contrast to that, Lao-Tse's warning that, "the people whose king talks a lot of peace, has no peace," sounded exceedingly pertinent to us. After floundering for a while in the field of philosophy, we realized that we needed a skilled hand to guide us, and we asked our Latin teacher, Joseph Huhn, Doctor of Divinity, to give us a course of philosophy which request he graciously accepted. Once a week, after school hours, we met with him in one of our houses or apartments and tried, in our youthful exuberance, to wear down his superhuman patience. He was a beautiful person.

At first, I expected that it would be Egon P., the brightest star in our class, who would ask most of the questions. Instead, this role was assumed by Menne B., one of the quieter students. Of course, we were not aware at the time that Menne was flirting with some Nazi ideas, nor that the rest of his family had already embraced the "new" creed. He was full of inner conflicts and uncertainties; it simply never occurred to us that his habitual mumbling was but a reflection of those ambiguities.

Another member of our philosophy group was Richard Sch. Without question, he was the most diligent student in our high school class. What he lacked in intelligence, he tried to make up by hard work. In that, he succeeded most of the time. Once in *Herr* Maler's music class, he was asked to recite some of Beethoven's major compositions. He got the opera *Fidelio* right, also the *Third Symphony*, the *Eroica*, but when he cited "the mass, *Mrs. Solemna*," he created one of the most devastating laughs that ever shook our classroom. It wreaked havoc with his reputation.

Richard was unable to resolve the problem of whether or not the Jews were actually different from other people such as the Germans, as though we were not also Germans. Every time he managed to think of a new angle to "prove" his theory to me who, in any case, saw little significance in that question, he would show up and belabor me with his latest brainstorm. Knowing that he was basically a "good" guy, somewhat confused to be sure, I always listened patiently to his fanciful notions until I found a moment when I could safely demolish them, and Richard would go home beaten like a dog with his tail between his legs.

Often he would come to my house and ask me to check over his compositions. His writing was as dry as a piece of leather belting dug up from some Egyptian pyramid. After thirty years, I learned sadly that a Russian shell had put an end to his life.

TEN
The Nazis are Coming

In 1932, in two successive national elections in Germany, there arose an extremely volatile voting pattern: The Social Democrats held steady at about six million votes, the Communists had broken through the seven million mark, and the Nazis, for the first time, had lost one million votes, coming down from thirteen to twelve million. When the monopolists realized that the two left parties could conceivably get together, settle their differences, and introduce socialism in a perfectly legal manner, they panicked.

Undoubtedly, some preferred a more middle-of-the-road type of government to the Nazis, even a social democratic one, as long as they were sure that their favorite brand of economic and tax policies were carried out, just as their English brethren across the channel had managed to do for an entire century. Some of them had little taste for that semiliterate, unpredictable, lowlife Adolf Hitler, and they looked desperately for an equation whereby this monster could be controlled. They found no such formula.

In their dilemma, they launched a succession of conservative coalition governments, each one more reactionary than the last, each one, hopefully, more placating to the ever more audacious Nazis than the last one.

Heinrich Brüning was the first such chancellor whose policies were beholden to those special interests. Coming from the right wing of the Catholic Centre Party, he was unable to line up a parliamentary majority as mandated by the Weimar Constitution. Hence, he had to govern largely by degree, with President Paul von Hindenburg's endorsement. In May 1932, after two years of unabated crisis, he was replaced by a stark reactionary, Franz von Papen.

One of von Papen's first steps was to legalize the Brownshirts, Hitler's paramilitary bandits. Soon overt and covert terrorism became the order of the day. Hardly a day would pass without the assassination of a number of political opponents.

It never became quite clear whether von Papen intended to weaken the Nazis' power by legalizing them or whether he was actually trying to strengthen them. His government too never attained a parliamentary majority and that is why he called for two national elections in 1932, in quest of broader support. Both missed their objective.

The shift of one million votes from the Nazis to the Communists was welcomed by a lot of sane people in Germany who hoped that, finally, the Nazi assault had lost its edge. Others, whose fear of communism exceeded that of fascism, turned panicky.

The circle of right-wingers around von Hindenburg, who was himself an old-time monarchist and militarist, tried to set up a broad national-front government of right-wing complexion to include the Nazis, too, before they would lose any more votes.

This task was assumed by General Kurt von Schleicher who carried out the last desperate attempt to forestall an exclusive Nazi takeover. After barely eight weeks of being chancellor, he had to go back to President von Hindenburg and admit failure.

These maneuvers came to naught because none of these political desperados had any mass support and, moreover, because the leadership of the trade union movement in Germany, with few exceptions, was too naive and too corrupt to organize any real resistance to the Nazis.

In the end, the monopolists with varying degrees of enthusiasm, talked President Paul von Hindenburg into appointing Adolf Hitler, now their "last white hope," as chancellor, with the proviso that he form a coalition government with the right-wing National People's Party. Their leader Alfred Hugenberg had for the longest time made a strenuous, if in the end unsuccessful, effort to hitch Hitler to his own wagon in order to use him to carry out his own favorite economic and political schemes.

Hitler quickly pledged his consent to Hindenburg's condition of a coalition, although he had no intention of honoring it. After a few months of an uneasy coalition, he kicked all non-Nazis out of his cabinet, including Hugenberg, leaving only Hjalmar Schacht as his finance minister and, in that manner, became Germany's dictator.

Today many people are still unable to unscramble the seemingly paradox phenomenon of fascist tyranny in Germany. One must surmise that it was the factional character of Germany during the last several centuries. It had been divided between two religious camps and two economic sections, one agricultural and the other industrial, mountains in the south and flatlands in the north, all differences that enabled the reactionary forces to play one group against the other, and to crush the repeated attempts at liberation which were successful in other countries. This generated the virtually traditional sense of frustration among the Germans and distorted their sense of proportion to such an extent that the fascists with such dubious issues as "the Jew" were able to lead them into the slaughter. Undoubtedly, anti-Semitism is not the key to the proper analysis of Nazism. However inhuman, it is just a sideline. In essence, Nazism is anti-German. Why? Because it produced such a frightful correlation between death and wealth in that country. The more people died, the richer the monopolists got. The Third Reich was not at all for the common man. If it had been, hundreds of thousands of the best German minds would not have been driven out of the country, or remained inside in icy silence. If the Third Reich had been for the common man, it would not have been for the rich, it simply would not have been the Third Reich.

The First Day

It was January 30, 1933, a Monday, when von Hindenburg appointed Hitler chancellor. I remember that day vividly. The sky was pastel blue, its hue paled by a thin overcast which the sun tried to penetrate with little success.

All morning, the German radio stations were blaring forth martial music, interspersed with frequent announcements of Adolf Hitler's accession to power and the composition of his cabinet.

We had just finished our luncheon. I joined my brother Theo who sat down near the radio to listen to the latest news that came over the wires. In order not to miss anything, he would nervously switch from one station to another.

Presently, we heard more than we cared to hear. Through the lace curtains, we watched a formation of about twenty men in the brown uniform of the storm troopers (SA), singing and marching through the street in an easterly direction, obviously headed toward the building that housed the *Fuldaer Zeitung*. This provincial newspaper espoused a middle-of-the-road course of Catholic Centre Party politics. It was clear to all onlookers that the SA aimed to terrorize the publishers of the newspaper to get them to acquiesce in the imminent takeover by the Nazis.

However, their song dealt with another subject. As they were passing our living room window, we heard the dreaded refrain: "When the Jews' blood splashes from the knife, things go twice as well." Barbarism with a musical twist and an ominous foreboding!

Soon, Theo switched to another station and, lo and behold, we heard some music that transformed the earlier, gruesome program into the most beautiful sounds of the heavens. What we heard was the first movement of Beethoven's *Violin Concerto*. It seemed that some radio station manager had defied the Nazi guidelines and, perhaps to gratify his own personal needs, decided to treat his audience to a "last hurrah" during this moment of universal horror.

We were both moved to tears, and my brother said in a state of transfiguration, "These beautiful sounds are the warrants of a happier future." Soon after the majestic finale of the concerto, he regained his composure, and he quoted one of his customers, an elderly peasant who was reputed to be a sort of down-to-earth philosopher in his farming village, that "things hardly ever turn out as good as one hopes, nor as bad as one fears." I was in much too skeptical a mood to surrender to such euphoria, but I was happy that, for a short hour, I could forget the bitter reality.

Why, Why?

The Nazis were indeed the German people's worst enemies. They were beholden to no one except the Thyssens, Krupps, Kirdorfs, Hugenbergs, Flicks, Wolfs, Vöglers and Schröders, the leading Nazi supporters among the Ruhr Barons and the major German banks. Not since the demise of the Feudal Ages, when total illiteracy prevailed, had there been a governmental power base as narrow as the one that Hitler set up, but now, with a German literacy rate of virtually 100 percent, a totally pervasive dictatorship with absolute censorship was needed the likes of which had probably never existed in all human history. Anybody inside Germany knew all the time that any overt opposition to that regime would bring about instant death. The concentration camps served not only as prisons for people hostile to the regime. Its other, and even more sinister purpose was to spread terror and the fear of God into the rest of the population.

From the moment that the conglomerate malefactors had managed to save their skin by making Hitler chancellor, the industrial, financial, political and military complex lost no time in building the most ferocious war machine the world had ever known.

To have a fuller understanding of that period of history, one must also realize that, before the Nazis were able to force foreign people into slavery and eliminate their middle classes, making everybody subservient to their master plan, they had to destroy the trade unions and their political leadership inside the Reich itself, and convert the German middle classes into willing economic and political tools of the monopolies, or physically do away with them altogether. This process was called "War Theater Inner Germany."

In order to realize the degree of trickery that the Nazis practiced, it is illuminating to trace the fate of one of the laws that Hitler promulgated for the welfare of the German peasants, or so it seemed at first, the so-called Law of Hereditary Tenancy.

Ever since the end of the feudal system, when the huge landholdings of the feudal lords and the church were divided up into small-scale farms and distributed to former serfs, there arose with every successive generation, the problem of further dividing up the already dwarfed holdings among all the male heirs of the original owner. Needless to say that, mostly within the short span of one or two generations, the remaining land had become too small to be subdivided further. Hence, the second, third and fourth sons were forced to leave the land and seek their luck elsewhere.

Only a few of these "excess" sons of peasants managed to find a marginal job in the new cities that arose about that time. Many others were less lucky and roamed the countryside as beggars and thieves. Many millions just starved to death and the hapless survivors found themselves stigmatized as vagabonds or outlaws being subject to the most severe perils of life and limb.

Ingeniously, with malice aforethought, Hitler called the German peasant the "Nation's Blood Source." Alas, as the war progressed, these peasants, fathers and sons alike, became indeed his blood source, the most numerous of Hitler's victims on the battlefield, his "cannon fodder." All that time, the profits of that unholy confederacy of Ruhr Barons, the big bankers, and their political and ideological flunkeys, buttressed by a *Reichstag* of insipid yes men, all exempt from paying any taxes whatsoever, soared in full proportion to the rivers of blood shed on their behalf.

Clever Ruses

Unquestionably, there were things that the Nazis undertook that looked good on the surface, and that have to be recognized as master propaganda strokes of that regime.

One of those acts which earned them countless supporters, was the creation of the para-military *Arbeitsdienst* (labor service). Many Germans were impressed when, all of a sudden, those millions of unemployed disappeared from the street. Every morning at seven o'clock, thousands of columns of young men dressed in workers' uniforms, with shovels slung over their shoulders, went marching and singing, or were driven by truck, to some predetermined location where they performed work, mostly building Germany's early autobahnen. When Hitler began his universal military conscription in 1935, it was easy for these work details to be converted to military cadres.

To many it was obvious that the prophet Isaiah's great vision of a peaceful society where "they will beat their swords into plow-shares and their spears into pruning hooks; nation will not take up sword against nation, nor will they train for war anymore," had been applied in reverse. Now it was the transformation of "shovels into shotguns," even before those *dumme Michels* by the millions were forced to march into the killing fields of the Red Army.

Another daring stroke that Hitler undertook, that to many Germans looked like a brilliant idea, was the occupation of the Rhineland. Under the terms of the Versailles Treaty, that part of Germany, forming a common border with France, was to remain demilitarized. Alas, when it happened, the world's protest was unexpectedly mild and as such wholly ineffectual. It seemed to us inside the Reich that the leaders of France and England were unable to look beyond their own noses.

The Versailles Peace Treaty also provided for a referendum of the Saar region to take place in 1935. Since this territory had been part of one German state or another even before the time of the French Revolution, when national consciousness became a significant political force, it was not surprising that the Saar voted for union with Germany.

What was, however, surprising and ominous to us was the high percentage of the pro-German vote. It sent the Goebbels' propaganda machine into a paroxysm of self-adulation for several weeks.

Many of us knew it then, and the world at large knows it now, that the official versions of the aims and purposes of these Nazi feats according to the gospel of Dr. Joseph Goebbels, contrasted wildly with the secret goals of these latter-day predators. Yet, there is no doubt that the perception of those events through the eyes of the unwary Hans and Liese, having long been scared to death by the ever-present terror of the concentration camps, strengthened the Hitler regime enormously.

The Roots of Evil

To a zealous historian it would seem easy to construe a direct connection between "Black Thursday" and its immediate consequences and Hitler's rise to power. However this approach is superficial and misses the substance of the problem. It appeared to many leading scholars of the period that the economic and political upheavals of the era, between the stock market crash in New York and World War II, signified nothing less than a major breakdown of the monopoly-capitalist system itself. For that very reason it also exacted its highest toll from the foremost exponents of that system—the United States, England and Germany.

Yet, in a strictly political sense, it was only in Germany where the economic tremors resulted in the cataclysmic displacement of the democratic type of government itself, while in the United States, England and most of the other industrial nations, the democratic system remained intact.

Sooner or later, the question arises as to why a substantial number among such educated and cultured people as the Germans allowed themselves to be so swayed, beguiled and double-crossed by those purveyors of the "big lie" and the "evil intent," that Hitler succeeded at all in bending the entire nation to his will and set the whole world aflame. How did it happen that he was so fanatically supported by about one-third of the German people? Another third were obviously too tired and indifferent to oppose him, and most of the remaining third were terrorized into submission by absolute, unrelenting brutality and terror. Could it be that the "don't know" people, as my mother had defined them, had joined the bad ones to the tune of one-third of all people?

To explain this perplexing phenomenon, one must recount the highlights of German history all the way back to the Reformation: the Peasant Wars, the Thirty Years' War, the War for Supremacy between Prussia and Austria, Napoleon's conquests and his ultimate defeat, the sad period of reaction, censorship and police informers between the Congress of Vienna of 1815 and the stillborn revolution of 1848, the failure to obtain a meaningful constitution, the rise of Bismarck and his imperialist aggressions, first against Denmark, then against Austria, finally against France, all victorious for the establishment, but unsettling for the people who had to pay in blood, tears and money, not to forget peace of mind, each event adding yet another tier of frustration, generation after generation, each adding another degree of national paranoia.

Each of these "glorious" ventures produced a host of perverted poets, clerics and theoreticians, sanctifying those calamities. Purloining their imagery from all kinds of questionable events and heroes of Antiquity and the Middle Ages, a mythology arose that convinced all the wretched, would-be armchair generals among the "people of poets and thinkers," many of whom could barely make a living, that France was "our arch enemy," and that the Kaiser had concluded a holy alliance with God Almighty, and that those two demanded unquestioning obeisance from their "subjects."

It is no doubt one of the most tragic aspects of the German destiny that the authors of this poetical and philosophical claptrap were by no means the small-fry, the fetid dregs of German literati that would soon be consigned to the ash cans of cultural and intellectual history. Quite the contrary was the case: they became the "celebrities" and were presented as role models, as just another part of the "elite."

In the early days of the empire, before World War I, when the cauldron first began to percolate, not many living rooms in Germany failed to display a picture bearing the legend "For God, Kaiser and Fatherland" showing one inspirational battle scene or another, interwoven with ribbons of the imperial colors: black, white and red.

Incidentally, at the end of the First World War, when the Kaiser was forced to leave Germany and settled down in the comfort of a Dutch castle, it took my father some time to move that memento of vapid patriotism from our living room into my parents' bedroom.

The intellectual miasma of the era was very well publicized and very well financed, and was thus forced down the mindless throats of many a German half-wit. Without its lasting effect, the Nazi movement would not have succeeded.

While the immediate effect of the Great Depression on our school life was relatively small, its impact upon business was calamitous. Every month, our sales would shrink a little more, and our ledgers would steadily grow larger, as more and more customers defaulted on their installment payments. When, in January 1933, the "Big Bang" happened, and Hitler came to power, my father and my two brothers, who were the three proprietors of the firm, had already planned to close the store and move our business into the large living room of our apartment in order to cut our overhead to a minimum.

But there were rumblings in our high school too. In the spring of 1931, we finished *Untersecunda*, equivalent to graduation from junior high. Ordinarily, this was the time when a few prospective clerks and some aspiring technicians among the student body were expected to terminate school with an associate degree. However, the year of 1931, for obvious economic reasons, had a drop-out rate of more than 50 percent of the total class. It was then that the school administration decided to merge the remaining students of the "A" and "B" into a single class, under our long-time principal teacher Dr. Stöhr.

What made this merger significant was the fact that, while in the original "B" class we had but one or two low profile Nazis, the "A" class had about ten with varying degrees of anti-Semitic propensities. Unquestionably, the number of "badies" in our combined class rose ominously. Suddenly we had lost our undisputed leadership and had to spend a great deal of our energies to ward off the brazen arrogance on the part of the new Nazis in our class towards a lot of values that we held.

Of course, even in the years 1931 and 1932, before Hitler's accession to power, we had skirmishes with some of our new Nazi classmates, but those we won easily, particularly since we had the tacit approval of several of our teachers, including Dr. Stöhr.

However, when the Nazis took over the government in January 1933, we soon found ourselves on the defensive. By then, fortunately, we had reached the conclusion that the great majority of the Nazis were cowards, possessed of an oversized inferiority complex that prompted their proverbial, strutting overbearance. Because of this psychological insight, we managed to handle them with a fair degree of equanimity. But every so often, especially when we found ourselves isolated or greatly outnumbered, things were never far from getting out of hand, and we always had to be on our guard.

It was also in 1933 and 1934 when we found that some of the Nazi teachers were coming out of the closets, some with an overweening sense of vindictiveness. The most aggressive and least sympathetic among those was undoubtedly our chemistry instructor, Dr. Westenberger, who was known among his non-Nazi colleagues as "Naziwest." He would deliver his lectures in an offensive monotone until, suddenly, he would spring a question on one of us four Jewish students in a manner that was patently calculated to catch us off guard. After a short while we caught on to his tricks and became better prepared to checkmate him. Another reason why his ploy failed was the conspicuous lack of applause for his cuteness on the part of the great majority of our classmates.

On the other hand, there was Dr. Huhn, our Latin and philosophy teacher. He was not only a scholar of the highest order, but a human being of unassailable principles and a heart of gold. As a priest, he held a high position in the hierarchy of the Fulda bishopric.

He was one beautiful person, and I was extremely lucky when he also became my personal friend. His rejection of Nazism came from a different rationale than mine, but it was so exquisitely simple that I had no problem adopting it. When we once discussed the German variety of fascism, trying to find out why it was really so bad, he said, "What do I think is wrong with that system? It has no morality." It gave me a lot to think about. Unquestionably, a dramatic polarization took place between the "goodies" and the "badies."

Interestingly, when the war was over, Dr. Huhn and I resumed our correspondence as though nothing had ever happened that could separate us. Unfortunately, when I went back to Fulda twice, for the purpose of visiting him again in person, I missed him both times. During my first visit he had just gone on a trip to a famous monastery in his beloved Rhön mountains. The second time I came to Fulda to see him it was just one week after his funeral.

Without a doubt, his presence in the school contributed greatly to making our lives more tolerable. However, there were other experiences which, occasionally, lifted our heavy sense of dejection.

ELEVEN
New Friends and New Teachers

When in 1929 we moved from the village of Flieden with a population of about 2,300 to the district capital of Fulda fifteen times its size, the change was not just a geographical one. In Flieden, I had known just about everybody, and had formed close ties with many. In Fulda, most people were strangers, my social life was much more diluted, much more anonymous, and in many ways less safe and self-assuring. This perception coincided with my adolescence and its crises. While I am certain that my commuting to the *Oberrealschule* in Fulda for several years made the transition somewhat less vulnerable, new problems arose nonetheless all the time. While in Flieden, I had carved out a certain central role for myself. Now in Fulda, I was overcome by the feeling of being a "dime-a-dozen" type. There were times when I had the sense of living in a vacuum and that life was passing me by. One of the results of this feeling of despair was a strenuous and conscious effort to build a circle of new friends. I started out by attending every meeting in town, concerts, lectures, what have you, and slowly built up a new set of acquaintances. In time, some of those proved unreliable and fell by the wayside. Others became my lifelong friends. Unquestionably, my morale was greatly boosted when I became aware that I on my part was considered worthy of other people's friendship too.

Two of my most unforgettable friends from that period were Walter Hirschheim and his elderly mother Betty. Walter walked with a pair of crutches and when outdoors, he got around in a wheelchair, for he was paralyzed from the waist down. But that aspect of his personality lost all significance as soon as you got to know him. For one, he was an excellent pianist and made his living by performing as a pianist at a variety of affairs.

Once Walter had made up his mind that you were a good listener, he would turn into an untiring teacher of music. In this manner, I was extremely lucky when he gave me a personal education in both classical and romantic music. A whole new world opened up for me. I soon was able to recognize every movement of Mozart's last ten piano concerti, many of his symphonies, his quartets and quintets, Beethoven's five piano concerti, his violin concerto, and many of his sonatas, trios, and quartets, his beautiful septet, and all his nine symphonies, movement for movement. They became all my own personal friends without which my life would have been deprived of one of its most precious dimensions. Between Walter, Betty and myself, we had endless discussions regarding the composer's meaning, be it Schubert's lieder or Brahms' boisterous symphonies, all that bloated my sense that I was "with it" to the bursting point.

During the Crystal Night roundup, Walter too was picked up and taken by bus to the collection point in Fulda but, being a paraplegic, was soon returned as a solo rider in the same bus to his horrified mother.

A later Nazi document, discovered after the war, tells us that both Walter and his aged mother were taken to the provincial capital of Kassel toward the end of August 1942, and from there transported to Theresienstadt where they perished.

It was in September 1933, eight months into the first year of Hitler's takeover of the German government, when a new teacher walked into the class room of the *Oberprima* (senior year) of the *Oberrealschule* in Fulda.

He was to be our instructor in a brand new subject on the curriculum, *Rassenkunde* (Race Theory), superseding both biology and zoology. His name was *Herr* Höhl. He was slim, bald and had a short nose which pointed skyward. His appearance, together with the awesome subject that he was to "teach" us, caused a lot of apprehension among the Jewish and some of the Catholic students. Who but a full-fledged Nazi would be teaching such a subject?

To our surprise, *Herr* Höhl turned out to be a "good guy," a friendly, warmhearted person, and his new assignment was no less distasteful to him as it was to us.

He looked the class over for a while, then he pointed at me and at Julius Hess, and said, "Will the two of you please stand up. I want everybody in this class to have a good look at these two fellows. As far as I can make out, they are the most Aryan types in the class." As a matter of fact, we were both Jewish.

The entire class burst out laughing. *Herr* Höhl realized his innocent faux pas and good-naturedly joined in the laughter. Come to think of it, it is true that we both have blue eyes. Lulu's wavy hair was medium blonde, mine was brownish, and we both had facial features that fell easily within the physiognomy that the Nazi idiots had officially designated as of the Aryan variety.

I must interject here some of the facts of life of our town Fulda and of our school. First of all, the area that comprises the Fulda bishopric had been a Catholic enclave in a vast ocean of Protestant land ever since the post-reformation settlement. As an isolated group of sorts, the Catholics empathized more than was usual with the Jews in their midst. Moreover, Bishop Damian was an exceptional human being who took his calling as the shepherd of His flock quite seriously, and would brook no breach of His stricture of loving one's neighbor.

In addition, our high school principal, Dr. Lauwartz, was not only a stern taskmaster, but he was also resolved as much as it was in his power, that the four Jewish students who had made it to the senior year, should be allowed to graduate come the Easter graduation time. Although he stood hardly more than five feet, he proved to be a giant of human values.

Then there was our mathematics teacher, Dr. Gotthard. Like most of our teachers, he too was a veteran of World War I. His mouth was somewhat slanted and his speech was slightly slurred, and we assumed that in the past he had suffered a light stroke.

Within the broad range of the political spectrum of the time, he was obviously a political conservative, a *Deutsch-Nationaler*, who had become impatient with the lack of efficacy of his own political affiliation and was developing a distinct affinity toward the Nazi party. Whenever he entered our classroom, he would posture himself in front of the students, stiffly raise his right arm and yell "Heil Hitler." However, despite his blustering gesture, we did not consider him to be anti-Semitic.

A few months before our graduation, we realized that he became more and more preoccupied with three particular problems among the last three years' math curriculum, one of calculus, one of spherical and one of analytical trigonometry, and it dawned on us that those three problems might have been selected for oral demonstration by some unlucky student at the forthcoming final examinations in front of all the professors most of whom were looking forward to this annual event as their own opportunity to show off in front of their colleagues with some tricky questions to the students. It did not take long until it became clear to everybody in our class that those were indeed the problems that would come up during the oral examinations.

I had realized for some time that I had irked Dr. Gotthard by hardly ever doing my homework assignment, although he rarely said a word about it. Suddenly, about three or four days before the scheduled orals, in a sort of Freudian slip, he pointed his finger at me and slurred the words "I'll get you yet." Those words and their obvious meaning were not lost on me. I spent an entire afternoon studying those three problems, no more, no less, until I knew them "cold."

Not surprising, the following morning, when they distributed those eloquent little slips as though they were Chinese fortune cookies, the subject matter on which you were required to hold forth being printed right under your name, I found myself the lucky recipient of one of those tags, and the subject was math. Uncannily, I was to elucidate the very three problems that I had studied.

I had about ten minutes to prepare my presentation. I jotted down the required three derivations in a jiffy on the blackboard assigned to me and when my turn came I began to rattle them off aloud, without the least hesitation.

"Why do you show us your back; it is not polite. Please, turn toward us." This was the only comment that was made, and it came from the principal, Dr. Lauwartz. Obviously, it was my lucky day.

In retrospect, there can be no doubt that the many millions who thought like Dr. Gotthard, who allowed themselves to be enthralled by the Nazi creed as a whole without necessarily subscribing to its rabid anti-Semitism, and in the end refused to oppose its excesses, must in some measure be held as responsible for them as the actual perpetrators themselves.

TWELVE
Volunteer

Paradoxically, our graduation from high school, in the face of this veritable bumper crop of difficulties, filled us with pride. It also confronted us with the towering problem of deciding our immediate future. My brother Theo, nine years my senior, had preceded me in the same high school in Fulda by as many years. He had been on rather friendly terms with a classmate who was the son of the largest machine manufacturer in town. They had kept their friendship up to the present day, and that was why, only two weeks after graduation from high school, I found myself cutting gears on an outdated and very temperamental milling machine at the factory of Wilhelm Hartmann (GMBH), not as a tool maker's apprentice, but as a volunteer.

The term volunteer requires some explanation. While the Nazis discouraged any form of employment of Jews by Gentiles from the very outset of their regime in January 1933, long before the enactment of the so-called Nuremberg Laws in 1935, no Aryan employer was even then allowed to enter into a regular apprenticeship contract with a Jewish employee. Those employers who had the fortitude to ignore the spirit of the Nazi guidelines, depending somewhat on the local political climate, got around the official line by designating the handful of new Jewish employees by the more acceptable term volunteer.

Actually, being a volunteer had several advantages. It was not common for a volunteer to have to spend a great deal of his time cleaning the machine shop floor, or putting tools away. These menial tasks were relegated to the apprentices. The typical volunteer was a high school graduate who intended to go on to a university to study engineering, after completing two years of practical work in a factory. That is why the foreman, the plant engineer and the work superintendent usually felt a kinship with him and tried to provide him with the best technical training.

This was also entirely true in my case. Moreover, since the three leading people in this enterprise, the owner, the work superintendent and the chief engineer, were anything but Nazis, I actually enjoyed many advantages in this position.

While my own goal at that time was to go to Palestine to help build up that country, there was another, non-Jewish, volunteer who intended to study engineering. Soon we became friends.

I would have had a pretty good time in this job, and learn a lot in the bargain, if I did not have to deal with the sudden, unexpected death of my father. He died of a massive heart attack on his fifty-ninth birthday anniversary, barely two weeks after I had started this job, four weeks after my graduation from high school.

Although I was never as close to my autocratic father as I was to my loving mother, my two brothers Julius and Theo, and my sister Elli, and a few cousins, the death of my father was the first severe shock of my life. By any standards, he had been the one pivotal center of my life. I was totally unprepared for this sad event and it hit me terribly hard.

After we buried our father I went back to work and it was then that I found out who my really good friends were. Number one was undoubtedly the master of the tinsmith department, Albert Vey. He took me under his special wings. For hours he would listen to my telling him about my childhood, my youth, even my first love.

Perhaps to show me that I was not really all that different from him, the most respected man in the entire plant, he would tell me about his own life, his philosophy, and his radical brother whom the Nazis had put into the KZ at the beginning of their regime.

From the moment that I had been assigned to his department, I realized that Albert Vey was not only a good tinsmith, but also a person of rare political and philosophical insight.

There was no doubt in my mind that he was too intelligent to have accepted life in the treacherous trenches of the First World War without questioning the rationales given by the imperial government and all the other official and unofficial warmongering mouthpieces and, perchance, think of better alternatives. While many millions in this world go through life and accept life's vicissitudes without ever questioning it, and other millions manage to escape reality altogether by becoming addicts of one kind or another, Albert was resolved to live his life in the rarefying air of optimal consciousness, and whenever the limits of his education threatened to inhibit his investigation, he would go back to the intellectual grindstone, so to speak, and educate himself in his new field of interest. He might be called a true autodidact.

During one of our many lunchtime conversations, he told me that he had recently read a book that contained famous quotations by famous people. He was particularly impressed by a military strategist, Karl von Clausewitz, who lived over a hundred years ago, and who had observed that "war is but a continuation of politics by other means." "When I read that," Albert said, "I understood why it was so easy for the German, French, English and Russian regimes to switch from talking politics and threatening each other to letting their armies march against one another." "Yes, they didn't give a damn about their people, the people just didn't count," I said.

Suddenly, I had a brainstorm. I turned to Albert, and in a low voice said to him, "If von Clausewitz defines war as continuation of politics by other means, might we not say that "Fascism is the continuation of the rule of monopoly capitalism by other means."

Looking around carefully, to be sure that we were not overheard, he said, "I think, you've got something there," repeating my "definition" a few times, nodding his head and pursing his lips.

Some contemporary smart alecks might wonder what possible purpose this intellectual ritual of formulating definitions of the stark reality of our time could have served. Yet to us, this was no exercise in futility. It was lifesaving. Getting a conscious and intellectual handle on the whereabouts of our situation was the only way of setting up boundaries beyond which the "enemy" was not allowed to intrude. They were our ideological barricades.

To a young person like myself, trying hard to sort out things, the worst emotional pain has a way of abating under the powerful influence of life's greatest consoler, time. Soon my father's death spurred me on to greater maturity and independence.

It was not long before my fellow volunteer, Karl, and I resumed the roles of an odd couple and, during work breaks, discussed all matters of concern to nineteen and twenty-year-old youngsters. There were several young ladies in the office who came under our frequent scrutiny, and we were flattered whenever our low-profile flirtations were rewarded in kind. There were also several attractive girls working at the assembly line, and we never failed to rejoice when we were ordered to repair their machines. Alas, being Jewish, I was precluded from going beyond the platonic stage, and Karl, on the other hand, had his own steady girlfriend.

After having been in this plant for almost a year, during which I had acquired a respectable body of mechanical knowledge in tool-making, metallurgy, sheet metal layout, blacksmith work and welding, so that I was frequently in demand by the various foremen to "help out" in their departments, I got into some real trouble with the headman of the nazified trade union local in the plant.

Herr Aul was a short, slim man of about forty. His bald head had the shape and size of an ostrich egg which someone had painted over in dark flesh tones, and which had a short, uptilted nose glued to it. According to Albert Vey's version, Aul's appointment as chief plant steward was the result of a compromise between a weak Nazi boss and a strong-willed plant delegation. It was obvious, *Herr* Aul was a terribly frustrated person, fully conscious of his inability to make friends among the workers, or even command their respect.

Predictably, to compensate for his shortcomings, *Herr* Aul was constantly on the lookout for any violations of the new rules and regulations pertaining to workers' rights and duties in Naziland. To Karl and me, he seemed to be a feeble reincarnation of Sergeant Himmelstoss in Remarque's *All Quiet on the Western Front.*

Rightly or wrongly, Karl and I had gotten into the habit of washing up five minutes before the bell rang, before noon and 5 P.M. Since we were volunteers and did not receive any wages, nor even any pocket money, it took Aul some time to decide whether the book of rules was applicable to us. The next day, again five minutes till noon, we ran up the stairs to the third floor where the washing facilities were set up. He followed us, and started to recite the "rules" in a manner that to him may have seemed quite reasonable, but to us sounded ludicrous. When the bell rang and everybody was coming up the stairs, he felt embarrassed and stopped his sermon. At once, some of the girls, who felt somewhat safer under the Nazis than the men did, started to rib him, winking their eyes at Karl and me to show us which side they were on.

When Karl failed to show the next day, I realized that I might have a problem on hand. Exactly at 11:55 A.M., under the watchful eyes of all the people on the floor, and in a spectacular display of adolescent indiscretion, I put my tools down and very slowly walked up the stairs. As soon as I turned the hot water faucet on to wash my hands, I realized that *Herr* Aul was standing behind me. He was clearly agitated, yelling at me that he had told me a dozen times that I was not to wash up before the bell rang, and he ordered me to go back down. I ignored him, but he did not let go. He cried out "Go, damn you, down with you, now!" shoving his right hand against my shoulder. I turned around, looked at him, and said calmly, "Don't touch me!" and went right back to washing my hands. He snarled and repeated his order, "Down you go!" and again pushed me with the palm of his hand. At that, I turned toward him, and hit his jaws, first with my right fist, then my left. He lost his balance and fell sprawling on the floor. That very moment the bell rang and everybody came up beholding the spectacle. I was scared to death for having embarrassed this official delegate of the superrace, but I recovered quickly when I saw that everybody was laughing crazily, all congratulating me. The prettiest of all the office girls came up too and planted a kiss on my cheeks in front of everybody.

For the next few days, whenever I had occasion to walk through the plant, everybody tried to catch my eyes and smile at me. It seems that, however thoughtlessly, I had done something that in the prevailing political climate nobody else would even have dreamt of doing. For a moment, I felt like a plucky Roman gladiator.

In the afternoon the owner called me to his office and lectured me sternly on the need to obey the rules, but he did not fire me. However, after another couple of weeks, the Nazis ordered the firm to let me go, a few days after they had removed *Herr* Aul from the factory and replaced him with a nice guy.

The one person who more than anybody else in the factory was absolutely delighted about my preposterous bravura was, of course, Albert Vey. Unfortunately, because he was under constant political surveillance, he could not afford to express his feelings openly.

Even after I was forced out of this job, Albert had a way of knowing of my whereabouts in Fulda, Karlsruhe, Hamburg, and again in Fulda. He was a remarkable person in every respect.

How often have I relived that ten-second chance encounter with him at the Fulda railroad station on that fateful afternoon of April 15, 1939, within an hour after I had received my permit for England in the mail. I had just bought my tickets to Frankfurt and London. The atmosphere at the railroad station was rife with the excitement of Armageddon impending. The only question in everybody's mind was whether Hitler would first go west or go east.

When Albert saw me coming out of the station while he was entering it to catch his commuter train to Vacha, he rushed by me and like a prophet of old, whispered, "Get out, get out fast. Do not wait another day!" and he was gone. It all happened so fast that I did not have time to tell him with supreme joy in my heart that having just purchased my tickets for England, I was in the very process of heeding his warning and give him a quick embrace.

After the war, when Germany was split right through the middle, I heard that he had become the mayor of his hometown, Vacha, an East German border town, barely fifteen miles from Fulda. However, when I once tried to visit him there, the East German army post would not let me drive past their road block, and I never saw him again.

Julius Marries Bella

It was just a few weeks before my encounter with Aul that my older brother Julius told me with an unusual degree of formality, that he had been introduced to an attractive lady whose name was Bella Friedmann, and he expected to marry her.

He told me that she was the daughter of the Jewish schoolmaster of Mainstockheim in Lower Frankonia, Siegward Friedmann and his wife Ida, nee Kissinger.

Before long, I received an invitation from the Friedmanns to visit with them, and I spent a weekend with the "new" family. Besides Bella, Siegward and Ida Friedmann had a seventeen-year-old pair of twins, a lovely, intelligent girl, named Lilly and her brother Manfred. I do not know how much Lilly's existence contributed to my weekend invitation. I liked her a lot, but not enough to fall head over heels in love. With great regret, I have to report that Siegward and Ida Friedmann as well as Lilly perished during the Holocaust.

While there, I also met Bella's grandfather, David Kissinger, a retired schoolteacher. He was a merry old soul who engaged me in many a philosophical discussion, while we took walks through the spreading vineyards in the Mainstockheim area of the Main River.

Nominally, David Kissinger belonged to the orthodox persuasion of German Jews, but his whole life-style revealed that he had his feet planted solidly in the twentieth century.

He had a charming sense of humor, and never took himself too seriously. I was glad to have the opportunity to be involved in a kind of philosophical banter with this revered scion of a notable family. It was decades later that the world learned that one of his grandsons, Bella's first cousin Henry Kissinger, had become the United States secretary of state, serving under the most despicable of presidents, Richard Nixon, and his successor, Gerald Ford.

A few weeks after the high holidays in 1934, Julius and Bella were married in a ceremony held in our large apartment in Fulda in the gloomy atmosphere arising from the fresh memory of our father's death, and the all-pervasive stench of Nazidom.

Böschen

It took me but a week to find another job with the Adam Böschen Steel Works, a small but highly reputable machine shop which was, not surprisingly, headed by Mr. Adam Böschen.

Herr Böschen had the pride and expertise of centuries of artisanship bred into him. He was a man of high moral motivation and a stern taskmaster. He had actually let it be known through the grapevine that he would like to have a young Jewish fellow for an apprentice, or volunteer, or whatever and, by that, he meant to do right by his Lord Jesus Christ.

I was lucky to be able to work for him. For one thing, he had the reputation of being the best master in town. "When you work for Böschen," people who knew him used to say, "you will get the best mechanical education." He was known as a friend of the Jews.

Besides myself, who was again called a volunteer, there were two apprentices, one journeyman and four masters, one of whom was his son, Adam Jr., and one of whom was Adam Böschen himself, the boss. With such a top-heavy organization, the Böschen shop had the reputation of being the leading machine shop in town. I was elated when, after a short get-acquainted period, he let me do the "hard" jobs that ordinarily would be left to the masters. One of those jobs was to re-sharpen the many chisels that were brought in. The trick was to do the whole job in one heat: after bringing the front end of the chisel to a cherry red, not any hotter, draw that end out to a flat bevel, soak one-half inch of that end in the cooling water for about a second, then quickly clean the tip on emery, or even on the concrete floor, and observe the change in colors as the heat was flowing back toward the tip. Just when the tip was turning to a corn gold, you had to immerse it quickly in the cooling pit. That produced the greatest hardness before it became too soft or too brittle.

Since these chisels were made of a toolsteel alloy, they could not be heated to more than a medium cherry red. It was, however, unprofessional to have to heat them a second time. Quite a trick, but under *Herr* Böschen's capable tutorship, I learned quickly.

It was about that time that Erwin Sittenfeld, the Zionist youth leader of the province of Hesse, "discovered" me. As one of the few young Zionists who had completed their high school education, I was just what he was looking for on his scouting tours through his territory. To get the young people to migrate to Palestine, and prepare them for a life of hard work and sacrifices, demanded more than just job training. It also required a basic ideology to help these pioneers overcome the many hardships that were bound to arise in a harsh and hostile land.

The more one knew about the geography, the native Arab people, economics, above all, Jewish history, old and new, the better one could be expected to cope with the realities of the old-new land.

Erwin Sittenfeld, though ten years my senior, became my best friend, and when we were later separated by the exigencies of the impending assault of the ruthless Nazi war machine against the world, it was as though I had lost a brother.

A Young Zionist

After a little more than ten months, Boss Böschen received a call from the Nazi headquarters in Fulda telling him that he had to let me go unless he wanted to have the delivery of his steel orders stopped. They wanted to shut him down, and they meant business. With tears in his eyes, Adam Böschen gave me the news. I packed up my tools and work clothes and left. As I crossed the cul-de-sac in front of his workshop, several of the residents waved good-bye. Suddenly, I saw *Herr* Böschen standing in the door and, throwing up his fist, he yelled to me, "Some day, we'll meet again under different circumstances!"

I met Adam Böschen one more time about ten years after the war. He was a broken man, hard of hearing, and spoke with difficulty, a pitiful image of his former self. His daughter had to interpret for him. I learned then, that a few months after he had to let me go, the Nazis had indeed shut down his workshop, and forced all the four masters, which included him and Adam Jr., to become foremen in the locomotive works of Henschel in the provincial capital of Kassel, to build tanks for Hitler's war machine. While in Kassel, Adam Jr. fell victim to a heart attack, and his grief-stricken father took his body back to Fulda and buried him there.

To me, the life of the Böschen family was symptomatic of the sad fate of the once proud and prominent class of German artisans under the iron heel of fascism.

When I reported the loss of my job to Erwin Sittenfeld, he began to take me along on his motorcycle to the outposts of his territory, and for a while, I felt like an appendage to his office. I met many people who worked in the numerous kibbutzim (centers of preparation), in their preparation for aliyah to Palestine, some of them very interesting people. I also met the leaders and groups of the local Jewish organizations in the hundred isolated villages and small towns in the state of Hesse where, for historic reasons, there existed many a small Jewish community. I gave lectures and had discussions on the various aspects of their lives. Sometimes, too, I would address the business people, or what was left of those, and make a pitch for contributions to some nearby kibbutz or to the Jewish National Fund. I discovered before long that the human spirit was capable of far greater deeds than the sarcastic, dehumanizing and demeaning Nazi propaganda wanted us to believe.

On an altogether different level, but no less trying for a twenty-year-old fellow, was the occasional meeting with some of the young beauties in the organization who were so love-starved that they were ready for any encounter, no matter how short-lived.

However foolish it may look in retrospect, at the time, I was not prepared to get involved in any sort of short-term relationship that could not possibly be part of a personal commitment.

Nevertheless, this kind of problem was little when compared to the very real problems that arose under the constant pounding on one's worth and self-esteem by the very clever and demonic propaganda machine that the Nazis had set in operation.

69

On one hand, the Führer Principle itself was a devilishly clever device to make the German people feel meek and subservient to their führer and führers, and eventually follow them blindly into the slaughter of the Second World War.

On the other hand, in their treatment of foreign people, all Germans were to act as part of the Aryan "super race" behaving with their familiar arrogance. Yet, when compared to the economic and political elite inside the Reich, the German masses were constantly reminded that they just did not measure up. This split-personality scheme worked exceedingly well for the master race elite of Krupp, Thiessen, Hitler, Göring et al.

If you were a Jewish youngster in the process of growing up in Nazi Germany, you had to arm yourself additionally against the onus of being rejected officially. Trying to be diplomat, psychologist and philosopher, being brutally frank, but always realistic and honest, I feel even today that, in the face of these fantastic handicaps, we and a hundred others must have done a pretty good job, for the truth is that we did get many thousands of young people away from the clutches of these Nazi beasts before the Holocaust started in earnest and destroyed nearly all those that an unkind fate had left behind.

The stark fact remains, however, that all of us were intensely apprehensive about our future, immediate as well as long range, and continuous person-to-person contact to discuss the multitude of our individual and collective problems was an extremely vital element in the success of our mission and for maintaining our sanity.

As the Nazis kept tightening the grip on our throats with unrelenting severity, emigration itself became more and more everybody's top priority. We had to watch with traumatic anguish, as the English government, which held the Palestinian mandate, kept allotting us fewer and fewer permits for Palestine in inverse proportion to the increasing urgency for Jews to leave Germany.

The United States, too, which for many prior decades had been the world's haven for the oppressed, now, in total callousness, started distributing just twenty thousand registration numbers for more than twenty times as many people, all desperate to leave Germany, Austria and Czechoslovakia.

THIRTEEN
Passover Incident

It was only a few days after I had been forced to leave Böschen that the Jewish community in Fulda prepared for the Passover Seder. In our house, both my brother Julius who, as the eldest, had now become the titular head of our family, and my mother took great pains to clean the house. In line with tradition, they removed all bread crumbs and other implicating bits of leavened food.

In those days before Passover, our culinary expectations rose to a high pitch and, at least a week before the actual Seder, our taste buds went wild in anticipation of the most delicious beef soup with matzo balls, and all the other goodies that would be served with the devotion and regularity that had become second nature to life itself, and that even the Nazis could not spoil.

Passover represents a beautiful combination of a religious ritual and a historic, even ideological breakthrough not only for the Hebrews but for all mankind. It was the first time in recorded history that a people, our people as it were, insisted that they no longer wanted to remain slaves and fought with great courage to attain their freedom, no matter what the cost. It is impossible to assess what this resolve of three and a half millennia ago did to other people in other lands and in other centuries up to this very day, to their inspirations and their achievements. What a guy this man Moses must have been to earn such a role for himself!

Passover falls on the two days of the full moon around the time of early spring, and every year, when we were sent to a place near the synagogue to burn whatever bread had still been found in the house, we were usually frozen stiff when we got back.

However, that penetrating cold only seemed to heighten our expectations, and would not go away until the middle of the Seder, when it is every Jewish housewife's ambition to serve her family the very best meal of the entire year.

This was also a time when thoughts about our town of Fulda shot through our minds, its history and how the Jews fared in those passed centuries of strife, wars and hostility, during the Crusades, the Black Death, the Thirty-Year War, the Reformation and the era of the Enlightenment that, obviously, had just ended.

We knew about the founders of the town, the famous Boniface who was sent from England to convert the German heathens to Christianity, those same heathens who later turned against him and hacked him to death, and his disciple Sturmius who lived in the first half of the eighth century, just before Charlemagne became emperor. Those early missionaries considered the few Jews in their midst as allies whose religion was in many ways the mainspring of their own. Later when the church became greedy and wanted to conquer the lands and land routes to the riches of India which had been blocked by the Mohammedans, they called for crusades. The populace, having no education, and being held in physical and mental serfdom, turned against the Jews with the promise of attaining greater glory, killed them, burned them, or converted them by force.

When the terrible plague, the black death arose, and about one-third of all the people of Europe perished, changing the face of the Feudal Age forever, they again turned against the Jews. They accused the Jews of having poisoned the water wells. The church leaders did nothing to alleviate the anger of the desperate population. Some actually incited the people against the Jews.

Fulda, too, had a tragic encounter with the Jews in its midst.

The first disaster, interestingly enough, did not occur at the time of a crusade, when everybody was agog and amok, but happened instead when Henry V, egged on by the founder of the (Un)Holy Inquisition, Pope Gregory IX ushered in a period of instability and lawlessness by trying—unsuccessfully—to overthrow the regime of his own father, that greatest and most enlightened ruler of the Middle Ages, Emperor Frederick II, the grandson of Barbarossa.

It was the last week of the year 1235, between Christmas and New Year, when a mob accused the Jews of Fulda of having slaughtered three children of a Christian family, in order to collect their blood for the "ritual" baking of matzo. The people went on a rampage setting fire to the stockhouse where many Jews had taken refuge. Thirty-two men, women and children died a fiery death.

In the ensuing centuries, when governments were supposed to have been more civilized, they alternately chased the Jews out of their territory, or allowed them to come back, either confiscating their properties on the way out, or exacting a heavy tax, or ransom from the lucky ones who were "allowed" to return.

It had become a sacred custom for the Jewish people in the Diaspora during the Seder to set aside one extra glass filled with the best wine in the house for the Messiah, a sort of bribe for him to come and deliver the Jewish people from their misery and lead them to Jerusalem, the city of their dreams. For the Jews believed deep in their hearts that the Messiah would put in an appearance, either when times were extremely good, and man had descended into a life of frivolity and sin, as in Sodom and Gomorrah, or when life was at its very worst. It never occurred to the faithful that the Messiah would have to undergo a multiple division of his own body to visit so many thousands upon thousands of places at the same time.

To add some further inducement to their plea for salvation, at the very beginning of the Seder ceremony, an invitation is extended to all hungry people to partake in the delicious meal of the evening, and at the same time have a chance to chime in the many songs of praise to God and to thank him for his many blessings.

Well, that night could have been just such a night. Of course, I did not know how everybody else around the table felt about the Messiah's intentions. To me, it was just a nice story, born in centuries of pain. Brother Theo surely did not believe it, while our mother probably did. I do not think that my brother Julius fully believed it, nor his new wife Bella.

We had just finished the first part of the Seder and were in great anticipation of our dinner, when the doorbell rang. Our housemaid Maria went to open the door and reported that two men wanted to speak to Theo, one of them dressed in the Brownshirt uniform of the S. A. (Nazi storm trooper).

In a show of solidarity that I had never been conscious of, but had taken for granted, the three male members of our family went to the living room, now converted to our store, to face those two men. In another minute, sister-in-law Bella joined us.

It turned out that one of the men was one of Theo's customers. He had recently bought a suit from Theo on credit. He now wanted his debt of about DM 200 canceled, just like that, and he requested a formal receipt for payment. While he sounded rather meek, almost embarrassed, his Nazi companion, clutching the dagger hanging from his leatherbelt as though he needed some extra encouragement, now accused Theo of having delivered a suit inferior to the original sample and, besides, he claimed that it did not fit.

Brother Theo, in order to call the man's bluff, asked him whether he wanted to return the suit and get his down-payment back. At that point the Nazi exploded into high decibels and yelled at Theo that he should just make out a receipt, or else. The "or else" was ominous; it could mean a number of things, from getting beaten up in the customer's village next time around, to having the store closed for good.

Although Theo was not at all religious, he pretended that he was not allowed to write on a holiday, but if the man did not want to pay for his suit, there was nothing that he could do about it.

With that, the two fellows left and at long last we began our dinner, each of us however with some deep thoughts.

There was no longer any question that Germany had fallen into the hands of chronic liars, ruthless assassins and machiavellian manipulators, and all our beliefs of a forward moving society with a majority of decent people had gone out of the window.

FOURTEEN
Karlsruhe

After about three months of acting as an itinerant youth leader, I was asked by our leadership in Berlin to go to Karlsruhe, the capital of the state of Baden, and take over the various Zionist youth organizations there, to succeed a young man who was about to leave for Palestine. They had found a job for me in a mechanical workshop, so I could continue my toolmaking and welding education.

One of the unexpected bonuses of my stay in Karlsruhe was undoubtedly my landlady, Mrs. Rosenfeld. I was tremendously impressed by the scope of her education. She could recite entire passages of Shakespeare from memory, and she widened my intellectual horizon considerably.

Baden is Germany's southwest border state. In the south, the Rhein River separates Baden and therefore Germany from Switzerland while in the west, it separates Germany from France. The people in Baden used to be looked on as some of the most provincial in Germany. They spoke in a dialect that was almost *schwyzerduitch*, and it took me a while to get used to it. Nowadays, under the impact of radio and television, and as a result of the huge transmigrations of people after the war, those differences have largely disappeared.

Between my job as a volunteer with the honorable firm of Speck and Pfeiffer and my duties as leader of the Zionist youth movement, I had little time for a social life. This was actually the first time that I had the responsibility for a number of groups of youngsters of different age and ideology. There was a group of *Werkleute* (work folks), whose credo it was to return to nature and live a simple, honest and fulfilling life on the land, grow food and raise a family, an idyllic concept a la Rousseau.

Their ideal to return to life's basics enabled them to identify with the Zionists, whose goal was, similarly, the creation of a nation which was close to the land, in contrast to the citified, urbanized and therefore unnatural life in the Diaspora. Here, it was only a matter of time, when the always latent danger of destruction would burst into the open. Since the *Werkleute* were small in number, they joined us as a group. Their members were of gentle disposition and easy to get along with. In former times, they used to be a branch of the once powerful German youth movement, and they taught us many new songs and games.

Another segment was the *Hashomer Hazair* (guardian of the land), whose ideology was derived from Marxism, but adapted to the specific situation of Jewish life in Europe and the future in Palestine. Their theoretician was a Russian Jew, Ber Borochov.

However, this group remained small and was confined to some few dedicated students of social science.

The bulk of the Zionist youth movement in Germany was comprised of the *Habonim* (builders), and the *Hechaluz* (pioneers). The *Habonim* consisted of schoolage youngsters, and the *Hechaluz*, as a rule, comprised those who were no longer in school, but were in some stage of preparation for a life in a kibbutz in Palestine.

A typical *Habonim* group numbered between five and twelve members, depending on local conditions and the availability of qualified group leaders. In Karlsruhe, there was a group of eight outstanding youngsters in their middle teens, each with strong leadership qualities, and our entire organization entertained great hopes for their future role in leading the national organization some day.

Alas, that day never came. As the fever heat of fascism in Germany grew toward its ultimate consummation, and everybody scrambled to get out, George, Erich, Jock, Manny, Walter, Mohrle, Myron and Gaby were cast to the four corners of the earth.

However in 1936 when I was in Karlsruhe, they were my group and each of them had his own group in turn. Without exaggeration, we could claim that we were the dominant element of Jewish life in Karlsruhe. Thinking back to this wonderful group of people even now, is still an inspirational, if whimsical exercise of the heart.

Before the year was up, just around Christmastime, when the streets in Karlsruhe were full of sleet and slush, the venerable Messrs. Speck and Pfeiffer, had an unexpected visitor from the Nazi Labor Front. He told them bluntly to let me go if they wanted to continue

76

to have their steel allotments delivered. That Saturday when *Herr* Speck paid me my regular five *Mark* weekly luncheon money, he pulled out his big blue handkerchief and amidst tears told me about the visitor. *Herr* Pfeiffer, too, got out his handkerchief and wept on my shoulder as we bid each other good-bye. The lesson that the two grieving oldsters presented at that moment was not lost on me. Again I collected my tools and my work clothes and rode on my old bicycle back to Mrs. Rosenfeld's. The following week I reported the loss of my job to headquarters in Berlin and I also called Erwin Sittenfeld in Kassel.

It was only a few weeks when I received a request to turn over the leadership in Karlsruhe to a couple whose emigration to Palestine had been delayed, and then go to Hamburg and take over the *Habonim* there. They intimated that in Hamburg there had been a rift between the leader of the *Hechaluz* and the leader of the *Habonim*, and they were siding with the former, and wanted me to replace the latter. I left Karlsruhe after a couple of weeks of helping the new couple settle down.

When I arrived in Hamburg, I was immediately struck by the sheer size of this city. It was easily the most attractive of the German cities that I knew. It had a cosmopolitan flavor, but the people were more standoffish, if less provincial than the ones I had encountered in Fulda, Frankfurt, Karlsruhe and even in Berlin.

My first task was to shake off Baden's southwestern dialect which had gotten mixed in with my original *Hessisch* and learn to speak a good *hochdeutsch*. Since I worked in a small shipyard in a little shipbuilding village outside Hamburg as a steelworker and welder where they speak *plattduitch*, my attempt to acquire a German without a dialect was frustrated. More than a month passed before I could engage in a decent conversation.

In the Köhlbrandwerft in Finkenwärder, my first job was to help update a small, 120-ton boat that a Jewish captain hoped to take to England and sell there for a profit. He was smart enough to take out enough insurance with Lloyds of London.

Outboard Toilet

In conformity with the international code for this kind of boat plying the ocean there had to be a second toilet and somehow it became my task to design and build this second toilet. The only specification that I received was that it should be of an "outboard" type hanging over the ship's railing.

Accordingly, I cut out a steel safety plate for the seat and bent up two flat steel bars for the two sideframes, forming hooks to hang over the railing. I connected the side frames by welding a steel bar across the bottom for foot support, and another bar across the top of the side frames, so the user was perfectly safe.

Oh yes, it was quite strong. What I forgot to take into account however was the fact that this gadget had to work equally well in a stormy sea and with seasick people as it did while the boat was sitting in the still waters at the dock. Too bad that I did not consider that a small ship tossed about in a blustery sea would raise havoc with the law of gravity, and that a person with an acute attack of seasickness might not find this gadget altogether as comfortable and safe as I had envisioned it.

Well, after more than a year in London, England, quite by chance, I met one of my former friends from Hamburg, who had been the boatswain on this ship. He gave me the following account:

When the boat, after several delays by the German government certifying agency, finally lifted anchor and reached the open sea to sail for England, a heavy storm arose, and the captain became the first and only victim of seasickness. He would lie in his cabin below deck and bark all kinds of inane orders to the crew above which were promptly ignored. On the third day, they sighted the English coast. Alas, at that moment, the boat crashed onto a sandbank and began to break apart. However, the crew was saved by the British coast guard and taken to London and the captain collected his insurance.

In this manner, by hook, crook or storm, the captain accomplished his goal of transferring his assets to England. Incidentally, my friend insisted that the outboard toilet was never used once and presumably has been resting at the bottom of the North Atlantic ever since.

FIFTEEN
Ever-Present Danger In Hamburg

While I was working at the Köhlbrandwerft, I attended an evening extension course in welding offered at the famous Hamburg Institute of Technology. As part of a little conspiracy, the type of which was rather rare in those days, between the lecturer, Professor Friedrich, the technician, *Herr* Müller, and myself, I managed to become enrolled. Since I already had considerable experience in practical welding and knew a good deal of math, physics and even metallurgy from my high school days, I made good progress. After just a few weeks, the two gentlemen were kind enough to recommend me for a job with the Hans Arp Company which was located near the Hamburg railroad station. I left my job at the shipyard and began to work for Arp.

Herr Arp was a rather serious-minded person, about thirty-five years old. Including myself, we were five mechanics building pipe structures for mounting motorized saws for cutting trees. It was a long-range government contract and for a while the Nazi government seemed oblivious to my presence there. Mrs. Arp, who later on became pregnant with their first child, took care of their small office.

One of the welders was a Communist who had been in the KZ for a couple of years. This man, whose name I believe was Bargholz, was a rather quiet type and kept pretty much to himself. *Herr* Arp did not seem to care much where a person came from or what his beliefs were as long as he put in a good day's work.

Another worker was a Social Democrat and sometimes I tried to involve him in some sort of political dialogue, but I found that he did not have any ideological depth.

One morning, this man did not show up and we were worried. He came in about 11 A.M. and in glowing terms reported to us that he had just subscribed to a plan to buy one of those Volkswagens that

Hermann Göring was going to build soon in the much vaunted, brand-new Hermann Göring Works, and which were supposed to be purchased by everybody for several years of weekly installments of five or ten *Marks*. He even gave us the date of his car delivery. Later, when I got him aside, I told him that I had the impression that he had just subscribed to the largest war loan ever undertaken in Germany and that I didn't think that he would ever see his car. He shrugged off my misgivings. I do not think he took me seriously.

After a couple of months, I was greatly surprised when *Herr* Arp started to pay me the regular wage scale for welders. This was particularly significant since I was living in a *Beth Chalutz* (house for pioneers). From then on, my weekly wages helped to provide a good deal of the total protein intake of my pals there.

Although I turned over almost all my wages to the treasurer of the *Beth Chalutz* in accordance with the prevailing honor code it was, nevertheless, the very first time in my life that I was earning a full salary and that filled me with great pride. It also further reinforced my self-image, so that I could perform my tasks with the *Habonim* in the face of ever-increasing irritations by the Gestapo, with a growing measure of self-confidence.

Our *Beth Chalutz* housed about three dozen persons, male and female, all of whom were learning some trade that would be useful in Palestine, although we always emphasized that one must never take one's specialty for granted, that in the new country one has to pitch in with just about any assignment.

Most of the young men who lived in the Hamburg *Beth Chalutz* trained for a life of sailors in Palestine and mostly worked on the tugboats of a Jewish tugboat company, the Borchard Line, that had not yet been aryanized. They were tough fellows with a keen sense of kinship and it was unwise to have them as enemies.

A few weeks after my arrival in Hamburg, the president of the *Beth Chalutz*, who had a Ph.D. in chemistry, left us and I was chosen president. I could not figure out, why they wanted me. Between my welding job and the leadership of the *Habonim*, I was a very busy fellow. I concluded that they had elected me because I was a "softie," and that they hoped to get away with all kinds of hanky-panky. I expected to run into all sorts of trouble, particularly with our seamen. I knew that at least one of our *Chaveroth* (female comrades) was pregnant, and that the fellow responsible for her state was not at all sure whether he wanted to marry her and our collective reputation was in jeopardy.

The *Beth Chalutz* was the object of frequent Gestapo visits. They really had a way of snooping around, harassing us, and constantly imposing new rules and regulations.

Despite these difficulties we decided to have a May Day celebration which we naively labeled "Spring Festival." Our program consisted of Beethoven's *Egmont Overture*, a monumental paean to freedom, Maasereel's magnificent woodcut serial *Sun*, my thirty minute lecture on the delicate subject of German fascism, some progressive poetry, Bach's *Toccata and Fugue*, followed by a "gala" dinner the centerpiece of which consisted of a meat and potato patty of two inches in diameter and one-half inch thick.

According to many in the audience of about ninety-five people, it was a "rousing success." We had no way of knowing whether the Gestapo had sent one of their spies or not. Looking back to the chances we had taken with this grandiose spectacle, we must have been plumb out of our minds. Strangely enough, nobody said a word.

The Jewish people in Hamburg, as everywhere else, were relentlessly being trodden under the savage Nazi boot. Still they had to find ways of restoring some sort of normalcy into their daily lives. In order to survive as individuals they were compelled to create their own measure of defiance. This was especially true of the adolescents in our organization. In fact, the pressures that the outside world applied without letup helped to forge a very unique fellowship and camaraderie among us that would have been unlikely in normal times. The ever-present danger hovering about us all the time also brought about a personal discipline that ruled our lives to a far greater degree than the Nazi laws could.

How otherwise would it have been possible to continue, month after month, week after week, day in and day out, to teach our youngsters the bare minimum of essential knowledge that they had to absorb in order to keep alive and to train them for a new and better life?

The Gestapo demanded that for every one of our group meetings, we fill out an application at least two weeks in advance of the event. We had to give the exact title of the subject matter to be treated. We had to project the exact number of participants within plus or minus two. Of course we had to give the place of our meeting.

81

As time went on the Gestapo would attend our meetings with increasing frequency. More and more we were forced to select some suitable passage from the *Talmud* as our forthcoming subject and as an added safety measure we would always have one of those books laid out before us just in case we were being surprised by one of those unwelcome visitors. The moment that the door opened we would switch imperceptibly from the ongoing subject to the posted passage in the *Talmud* according to our notification.

Half the time we did not have the right number of participants and we had to leave our designated meeting place for a secret one.

The Gestapo could have used any one of those "transgressions" as a subterfuge to close us down. It was tough, believe me!

Adoration

As the Nazi rein of oppression became more and more stifling our *Beth Chalutz* developed increasingly into a social center for young people who had simply no other place to go.

Frequently their home life was chaotic. After years of forced unemployment their family resources were drained and often had to be supplemented by the Jewish community chest that was already strained to the limit. The pressures to leave Germany in the face of the world's refusal to accept them, raised havoc with a normal family life. Nagging arguments were the order of the day.

It was, therefore, not surprising that on any given Friday or Saturday evening our *Beth Chalutz* had perhaps three times its normal complement of people, mostly young ladies who hoped to find a boyfriend to share their misery.

I was always impressed by the high class of those visitors. Most did not come in search of a short encounter, but like millions of other girls and fellows the world over, hungered for human companionship. Needless to say, we ourselves were also looking forward to these weekends with similar expectations.

Among our many visitors, one girl in particular paid a great deal of attention to me. She would show me news items that she had cut out from newspapers such as the *London Times*, she would recite poems to me or just talk to me. Yet for many a month I did not consider our relationship as anything more than friendly. My god, she was only fifteen years old and I was twenty-two!

Ruth R. was exceedingly pretty. Her golden locks framed an oval face with a pair of deep blue eyes, full lips and a slightly courageous nose. Her figure conjured up associations with the famous marble sculpture of Aphrodite that Schliemann had dug up in King Minos' palace in Crete half a century earlier.

Despite my subconscious refusal to go any further with this erotic fancy, my provincial naivety experienced a tremendous jolt when Ruth told me that to celebrate her 14th birthday anniversary, a year ago, her parents had let her go on a bicycle trip with a "boyfriend" several years her senior. They stayed overnight in a tent and it was then that she lost her virginity. Her beau left her immediately and she had been "without a man" ever since.

Despite the titillating character of the subject matter I decided to treat it as just one more personal problem that I had gotten used to facing in a complex world. But I was wrong.

Unrequited Love

Well, summer was coming and we prepared for two weeks of summer camp on a large Jewish-owned farm a mile from the Danish border. We had about sixty kids between twelve and twenty years old, five group leaders, one cook and one business person. We also had engaged several "experts" to come for a day or two and lecture on their specialties. Being very large, the farm was isolated, and we felt rather secure there. The camp proved to be a success.

Of course my little friend Ruth was there too. She had come with a half a dozen of her girlfriends whom she had apparently briefed about "our relationship" whatever that might have been. Still it was disconcerting to me and to some of the older participants in the camp that Ruth and her friends would routinely sit right next to me in what we called the assembly hall which in reality was a large barn floor where we ate or had one of those lectures that I had to chair. Ruth was a frequent participant in the discussions following these lectures and she proved to be much more mature than her chronological age would let one assume.

After a few days in camp, it seemed to me that for whatever reason, she was calming down and her goo-goo eyes had dimmed a wee bit until one evening, I saw her crouched in the far corner of the barn floor holding her head between her hands and crying bitterly. Walking over to her, I put my hand on her head and in a reassuring voice asked her what the matter was.

She looked up and blurted out, "Why do you make it so difficult for me?" Well, I must confess that, having faced up to many surprises in my life with a fair degree of composure, I was totally baffled by this one. I suddenly realized that I had become personally involved in a confrontation between what I perceived as a very vulnerable girl of fifteen, and a twenty-two-year-old fellow with very normal and natural feelings.

At the risk of producing a short circuit in the ever enterprising and extrapolating fancy of some of my readers let me hasten to add that nothing, absolutely nothing, happened during the remaining days in the camp, although I cannot deny that it required an infinite amount of patience and restraint on my part.

To keep things in their proper perspective I must add however that with the exception of my little friend Ruth, I did not at all miss out on the pleasures and, sometimes, the pains of a young man. Almost without exception, my encounters were with "normal" partners with a surprising minimum of neurotic afflictions. Yet none of these were of a lasting nature. The pervasive instability of the time did not favor such a weighty decision. Once, I must admit, I did have an affair which bore a strong affinity to Shakespeare's *Taming of the Shrew*, except that I did not feel duty bound to play Petruchio, the tamer of the shrew. I doubt if this particular lover of mine was capable of shedding her egocentric and narcissistic bondage even when surrendering to the final quivers of ecstasy during the moment of ultimate joy.

SIXTEEN
Several Kinds of Hazards

The end of the camp had been set for September 2. This gave us a chance to have a campfire celebrating International Labor Day which fell on the first, a Wednesday.

All day Tuesday, a volunteer committee collected fallen trees and firewood, and built a stake, twenty feet high, in the middle of an open area of the farm that had been reaped clean prior to our affair. Another committee had scrounged up a gramophone and several records, some short stories and poems appropriate to the occasion, and the program was rehearsed a few times. We also collected what was left of our store of food and cookies and set up a stove for making tea.

As the sun began to go down, we made our way toward the campfire place, and settled down in two large concentric circles.

After we had started the fire and had played some inspirational music, I rose and tried to explain the significance of Labor Day. Although almost all of us came from the middle class, I said it would not be long when we would be part of the working class, and then we would appreciate the importance of sticking together.

While the German government tried to discredit the importance of the international solidarity of the working class at all cost, and make fun of it, this thought held one of the most powerful promises for our future. After this short talk we began to eat, drink and sing into the cool evening breeze. That was the end of our summer camp.

Early next morning, two trucks arrived and took us back to the unromantic world of reality. Although the trucks took no more than two hours to reach Hamburg, it took us another two hours to let all the people off in the various parts of the city and the suburbs.

When I finally returned to the *Beth Chalutz* and took my things back to my room which I shared with two other *chalutzim,* lo and behold, there stood my friend Isidor Heil. What a joy to meet him again!

Somehow, he had gotten my address from his family in Flieden. He behaved as though we had never been separated. He held a large bag under his arm. It contained a tremendous loaf of bread and a kilo chunk of butter. After that, he visited me every other weekend, and made the same "bread-and-butter" delivery to us. Some guy!

Once when Isidor Heil came to bring us the usual goodies, he took me aside and asked me if I might be good enough to go shopping with him in a Jewish haberdashery store to help him buy a tie. While I would not have refused to accompany him to the moon if he had ever asked me, I found it rather strange that he needed a companion for buying as prosaic an item as a tie.

He confessed to me that he had been attracted to one of the young Jewish salesladies in the store and wanted to get to know her better and he was sure that I could help him with this scheme.

Well, at that moment, I was reminded that whenever I was required to send one of our young girls or fellows to some kibbutz where some eligible, unattached young persons of the opposite sex lived, so that there was a chance that they might get together, some wise guy would invariably ask me: "Playing God again, eh?"

Issy must have sensed my reluctance and he mumbled something like, "I was just kidding." He never mentioned it again.

For one thing, he was married to a very lovely and brave lady. For another, he would have courted disaster had the Gestapo gotten wind of this.

Fall came and went, and winter made its entry with a lot of rain and sleet. The last thing we managed to do as a group of about ten *chalutzim* was to attend the annual St. Pauli festival at the Dome Plaza.

There was a multiplicity of stands for food and drinks. There were peep shows, magicians, palm readers and animal performers. There were games with trap shooting, miniature bowling, ring catching, and one game called *Hau' den Lukas* (Strike Luke). The latter consisted of a high track with a puck that, when you hit it hard enough with a wooden mallet, would climb up all the way to the top and strike a bell. The prize was a doll made of velvet.

During my days as a blacksmith in Fulda, I had acquired the quick knuckle motion that comes in handy for that exercise, and I bought three tries for twenty-five pennies. Then I lunged out and came down as hard as I could on the puck. The thing ran down and around the curve and up, striking the bell, but it kept going up slipping out of the rails and falling to the ground. The owner gave me my prize, and returned the twenty-five pennies too begging me to let it be at that and not go through with the other two tries. Since I did not need that kind of a doll I presented it to one of our *Chaveroth*.

While this outing was a display of gallows humor in the face of total adversity, it was also the last time a number of us in the *Beth Chalutz* managed to carry on a public social function as a group. All through the spring of 1938, everybody became more and more preoccupied with his and her own salvation.

In the beginning of April, Boss Arp was forced to go through the same sordid routine that my previous employers had to undergo, and his now more visibly pregnant wife handed me my last paycheck.

Within a few days an order arrived from our Berlin leadership to go there and attend an emergency conference. While our leaders talked and talked, they were stymied and had no solutions to offer. The situation looked bleak. To top it off, I ran out of money for my return ticket and I decided to hitchhike back to Hamburg.

I wanted to be smart so I carefully removed any papers from my person that might have identified me. After all, I was of military age and they could have suspected me of being absent without leave. Actually, it was a dumb move.

Sure enough, after a kind traveling salesman had already driven me to within fifty miles of Hamburg, at 11 P.M. that night, I was still sitting on a curbstone in one of those Godforsaken little towns on the roadway hoping that I would be picked up before the night was up for that ridiculously short stretch to Hamburg.

A few cars passed, but none stopped. Suddenly, I heard the heavy boots of a policeman coming around the corner. He walked straight up to me. "Well, what do we have here?" he asked. I told him that I was waiting to be picked up by a car. He explained to me that hitchhiking was unlawful and took me to the police station.

Without further ado, I was fingerprinted and photographed from the front and the side, just like an ordinary criminal. I gave them my name and home address but I had no papers with me to corroborate my identity. They put me in a cell overnight and in the morning, they took me to the local army garrison where I was imprisoned on suspicion of having deserted the army.

I did not know it then, but they had sent my photos to the police in Fulda for verification. After I had spent three days in the guardhouse, they received a telephone call from the chief of the Fulda police, *Herr* Berend, whose son was one of my brother Theo's friends, confirming my identity and also that I was Jewish.

The military officer who let me out was a nice fellow. He apologized for my detention and added that I could have avoided all this trouble if I had only told them in the beginning that I was Jewish. There you go. Almost immediately I was picked up by a car and the driver let me out right in front of the *Beth Chalutz*.

As soon as I showed up in our kitchen to say hello to the girls working there that day they handed me a little slip of paper that read, in very neat handwriting, that I was to report at once to the deputy chief of the Gestapo region northwest, at the Gestapo headquarters in Hamburg.

Well, the old butterflies came back with a vengeance. I figured that if I split the Gestapo would immediately close down the entire organization. If, on the other hand, I do go there, they'll arrest me at once and send me off to the KZ. Some choice!

Why I decided to take a chance, I have never quite been able to figure out. Early next morning, with a heart as heavy as lead, I made my way to the Gestapo headquarters while pondering my prospects during the impending twenty-four hours. I knew that this fearsome brick building that had walls one meter thick, and vaulted, casemate windows that were too small for anybody to escape, was not just used as an office building, but its basement served also as the chief Nazi torture and execution chamber for the province, and in that capacity, it was known to be a very busy place.

I went inside through a heavy door and giving my name to the information officer asked for the deputy chief's room. He picked up the phone and then directed me to a room on the second floor.

I knocked at the door and entered the room. The deputy chief was sitting behind a desk and greeted me with the old German *Guten Tag*. Then he asked me whether I knew him. I looked at him and said, "No, I do not know you."

"But I know you," he said, "and I kind of like you."

This sounded so outlandish to me that I had to strain all my senses to keep in control. Then he went on to tell me that he had come to my group meets repeatedly and, somehow, had taken a liking to me.

So when the "old man,"—he pointed to the next room, where the chief himself had his office,—wanted to cart me off to the KZ, he had proposed to him that they should simply kick "that bastard" out of Hamburg and be rid of him and, strangely enough, he bought it.

"But," and he shook his finger, "do not fight us; you will lose. We give you twenty-four hours."

At this crazy turn of events, I thanked him and assured him that he would have nothing to worry about my timely departure and left. Too bad that I did not have the presence of mind to catch his name. I went back to the *Beth Chalutz,* packed my satchel and took the first train to Fulda.

I realized later that I must have been in severe shock for leaving Hamburg so precipitously, without at least making an attempt to bid my friends farewell and let them know where I was going.

Ruefully, I was thinking of Issy, Lucy, Naomi and many of my other friends whom I had left behind. Above all, the thought of forsaking my sweet little friend Ruth has never quite left my mind.

As for Isidor Heil, it was four decades later that I located him in our native village of Flieden to which he had retired and where he had built a handsome house for himself and his wife. As soon as he recognized me, he broke into uncontrolled sobbing. For a while we were both crying on each other's shoulder like two babies in distress. After we had composed ourselves he told me that he had gone to the *Beth Chalutz* on the day I had departed and was told by one of the *Chaveroth* that I had been summoned to the Gestapo that morning and they had not heard from me anymore after that. Issy immediately concluded that the Gestapo had given me the usual, well-known "treatment" and started to mourn for me.

He then went on to tell me that he had to fight in Hitler's army in Russia and was a Russian prisoner of war for several years, he who had also been a soldier for the Kaiser in World War I.

He then told me that recently he had surgery for cancer of the stomach, but that he needed another operation shortly. However, his condition did not seem to deter him from relating to me a lot about his life in Hamburg, in the army and then in Flieden. He appeared to look better than his physical condition would lead one to expect. Of course he was still my very dear, old Issy.

At this point, his wife excused herself to go to the kitchen and prepare dinner. At once, Issy asked me about Tante Emmy's fate.

I told him that she had gotten married in Bergheim/Waldeck to her brother-in-law, after his first wife, Emmy's sister Bella, had died in childbirth. Bella's surviving baby boy, Jonny, grew into a handsome and intelligent youngster. Emmy had two beautiful children of her own, Kurt and Ruth. The entire family perished in the Holocaust. At this, Issy turned to me and tearfully said, "You know, I was once in love with your Tante Emmy."

It was no more than four weeks after our emotional farewell that I received a letter from his wife, containing a copy of his obituary. *Sic transit gloria mundi!*

SEVENTEEN
Encounters

When I came home to Fulda I sensed at once what, until then, I had always considered "my home," had changed. True, my mother was still there administering to her family. Her happiness to see me again in these worrisome times was well-nigh complete. She still did the cooking, sometimes even the cleaning of the dishes, but the equilibrium had shifted to my sister-in-law, my brother Julius' wife Bella.

Since I had not lived in our apartment for any length of time for the last three and a half years, and so many important things had happened everywhere, I did not ascribe any great significance to that subtle change at home but it hurt me to notice the unmistakable air of animosity between my mother and my sister-in-law.

All my life I had never known anybody holding a grudge toward my beloved mother, and I was considerably saddened by the thought that she too must feel the hurt.

Before long, I heard that the Jewish Training School in Frankfurt was looking for an instructor in sheet metal layout and welding and I applied for the job.

I went there for an interview and I got the job. However, due to some severe fiscal problems, I was told that this job was not going to be available for a couple of months. Hence, I went back to Fulda waiting to be called. At that moment, I felt a distinct kinship with Peter Schlemihl—I had no job and no money.

While I was leading a life of suspended animation, history, at least on a small scale, did not entirely ignore me.

One afternoon, at the end of a busy day trying to persuade some rich Jews in Fulda to make a commitment for a larger than usual contribution to the Jewish National Fund, I was walking down the wide sidewalk of the *Bahnhofstrasse* toward our house, when I heard a half dozen whistles blow from several directions.

Before I was able to analyze this unusual occurrence, about ten fellows on bicycles, none of whom I recognized, approached, encircled me and followed my gait down the street. They started to taunt me and steadily closed in on me leaving me less and less space for walking. Of course I realized that it was just a matter of seconds before they would stop me completely and then—who knows what. In a desperate move, I grabbed the two bicycles nearest me and pushed them away with all the power at my disposal, and they felled the others like dominoes. I started running down the street toward my house as fast as I could to gain as much of a head start as possible. Just as I was reaching the intersection with the *Rhabanusstrasse* where I lived, I saw my brother Julius coming from the other side of the street, also on his way home.

By that time, of course, those bicyclists had rallied again and were now right behind me. It took Julius no time at all to realize what was going on and, quick as a wink, he joined me and just as I had assessed the Nazis much earlier as a bunch of cowards, they were afraid of tackling both of us at the same time and they just followed us. When we arrived at the heavy wooden door of our house, Julius rushed to open it letting me in first. But as he was following me one of the fellows kicked him in the behind and we slammed the door shut.

Naturally, we did not think that that was the end of the episode. Sure enough, right after the sun went down and the street lights came on, we noticed that perhaps twenty youngsters had gathered in front of our ground floor apartment. Since the wooden, outside shutters were down, we carefully opened the window and listened to their debate as to what to do with me. Surprisingly, I had one defender in the crowd, and he happened to be a foreman with a moving company down the street, the same company that had taken care of my brother Theo's move to America a few months earlier.

We used to consider him a rabid Nazi, but now he kept asking the others what they would have done in my place and then asked them to go home. I am sure that his courageous intervention saved me from great harm.

But I did not trust the others. Right after they had disappeared, I called one of our family friends who lived a couple of blocks from us and asked whether I could spend the night there. I am still thankful to Mene K. and his wife for their selflessness.

It was only a few days after my experience with those bicyclists when I was again walking down the *Bahnhofstrasse* to go home. It was late and I was walking on that part of the sidewalk where large trees spread their branches umbrella-like over most of the street. Suddenly, out of nowhere, I was joined by a man in S. A. uniform whom I recognized as my barber who used to cut my hair. I had no time to express my surprise about this unexpected encounter, for this man whom I had never suspected of being a Nazi, pulled out his dagger and held it just a few inches from my throat and said in a raspy voice, "I am going to kill you!" Somehow, I was not terribly frightened. I knew that he was slightly taller than I was, and heavier, but I thought that if he should be serious and go just one step further, that I would knock the dagger out of his hand and box him to the ground. Surprisingly, he left me as quickly as he had first approached me. I thought that perhaps he had suffered an attack of temporary insanity. Strange people, those Germans!

EIGHTEEN
Carol and Munich

While I was waiting at home for news regarding my new job, I was still making phone calls to the *Habonim* headquarters in Berlin pushing for a permit for Palestine. Every time I called them, a different person seemed to be in charge and I became alarmed. I could not help feeling that our leaders were helping themselves to the few available permits. It irked me to realize that while I had been the leader of the *Habonim* in the second largest city and organization in Germany, I was denied one of those precious permits. Time was indeed getting short. In my desperation, I started to send letters to various relatives and friends in several countries asking them to try to get me a visa to anywhere.

It was about that time that my brother Theo introduced to us Elsie Heim as his fiancée. Elsie and I hit it off. Whenever she came to Fulda she was always ready to help out with the work in the house and my mother who was getting on, appreciated that.

Theo's and Elsie's wedding took place in the only Jewish hotel left in Frankfurt. While almost all the members of both families came to the wedding, my sister-in-law Bella did not feel well enough to participate. However, she told me that she had invited a young lady from her own hometown of Mainstockheim who had been working in an orphanage in Frankfurt as a kindergarten teacher for over a year.

Soon after the ceremony started, I heard the rear door open and, looking back from my front row seat, I noticed a most beautiful young woman taking her place near the entrance. I looked again, and in one of those irrational and wholly unpredictable attacks of intuition that seemed to beset me occasionally in the years of my post-adolescence, I thought, if that young lady is as intelligent as she is beautiful, I am going to marry her.

At the end of the wedding ceremony I asked somebody to introduce me to the young lady, Miss Carol Lomnitz, and soon we were engaged in a lengthy conversation. Almost at once it became clear to me that the condition that I had set, the one about her being intelligent, was met and I resolved that from that day on I would try very hard to get to know her better.

Ever since my return from Hamburg I had no income whatsoever and I had to rely on handouts from my two brothers. It was usually Theo who "granted" me a weekly pocket money of two or three *Marks*. It was not that he was stingy. On the other hand, I would not consider him the epitome of generosity, either. The stark fact was that, in the fall of 1938, in the face of the continuous harassment of our would-be customers by the Nazi bandits, the store and therefore our income, had virtually ceased to exist.

For this reason too our "courtship" was largely limited to a heavy trail of correspondence. I was elated by the temporary re-awakening of my long-suppressed poetic talent, and I sent Carol long letters of prose interspersed with some lyrical poems, in total incongruity of the spirit of the realm that was barreling forth with seven-league boots towards the ultimate catastrophe of war and woe. For the moment, we were living in an exquisite world of our own, our correspondence reflecting the beauty of our past lives and our esoteric dreams of the future.

There was no question in our minds that, if at all possible, we wanted to leave Germany in a legal manner, preferably with some sort of foreign permit or visa. Still, to play it safe, every time Hitler was about to let go with one of his ominous and raucous speeches, I traveled to Frankfurt in order to be near some easily accessible border.

September 29, 1938, was just such a day. Carol and I met on the *Kaiserstrasse* right outside the main railroad station, opposite one of those newspaper kiosks, and we were debating whether I should try to cross the nearby Belgian border that night or the safer Swiss one which was of course much further away.

Suddenly, we noticed that a new newspaper edition was placed against the kiosk's display window and, in great excitement, we read the headline that announced for the next day what later came to be called the Munich Conference. This meant that there was another reprieve in store for us, no matter how fragile.

The following day, September 30, the "Four Horsemen of the Munich Apocalypse" met, and produced the greatest calamity this side of Eden. Chamberlain, Daladier and Mussolini agreed to let Hitler take Czechoslovakia, as long as he kept going east, a lesson that was not lost on the wily Joseph Stalin.

One person who put totally false hopes in Chamberlain's easy consent was Adolf Hitler himself. He was most assuredly fooled by taking Chamberlain's endorsement of his own *Drang nach Osten* seriously. He and his half-bright foreign minister Ribbentrop forgot that in England they had a democracy and when the time came the English people would not condone Chamberlain's cop out and kick him out as prime minister in favor of Winston Churchill.

So we did have a reprieve; we knew that it would not be a long one, and we intensified our efforts to get out.

One of the best hopes for helping us get out before the rushing deluge hit us was now my brother Theo who, with his bride Elsie, had migrated to the United States right after their wedding.

Even while returning back to Fulda by train, I was setting up a letter to them, this time in English, putting down my thoughts of what might lie in store for us in the immediate future. The gist of my letter was that because of Chamberlain's and Daladier's abject surrender to Hitler's demands for Czechoslovakia, there was to be no shooting war for the time being and that, paradoxically, the more bloodthirsty segments of the Nazis would let their frustration out on some readily available surrogate victims, the Jews.

By one of those unpredictable coincidences that affect peoples' lives, my brother Theo was carrying that letter in his pocket when he visited the posh New York City apartment of the prestigious American lawyer Louis S. Weiss, in order to bring regards to the Weiss family cook from her German parents.

When the cook introduced my brother to Mr. Weiss, Theo let him read my newly arrived letter. It seems that my analysis impressed Mr. Weiss and he decided to execute an affidavit of support for me for my early entry into the United States. Alas, history's roller coaster had planned a different scenario for me for the time being.

Before long, Himmler and Goebbels went to work to find a plausible rationale for their planned wholesale assault against the Jews of Germany. A chance event in Paris was to provide them with that opportunity.

NINETEEN
Crystal Night

A few weeks after returning to Fulda, I received the long-awaited call from Frankfurt to start my job as an instructor in sheet-metal layout and welding. I went back to Frankfurt on Sunday, November 7, 1938, to stay temporarily with Tante Becka's sister, Röschen, and her husband, Levy Stern, until I could find a permanent home.

The following day I started my job as a welding instructor in an atmosphere of indescribable tension. Just ten days earlier, on Friday, October 28, the Gestapo had scooped up tens of thousands of Polish Jews in Germany, packed them into trucks and trains and let them out at the Polish border. There they chased them into the no-man's-land between the two countries, and left them to their own devices without food or shelter.

Among those people were several of my former classmates and friends with whom I had shared years of my life. How sad it was that nobody, neither Poland nor France, nor England or the United States, came to the rescue. It looked like an ill-omen of worse to come.

Among the deported were a couple, Mr. and Mrs. Grynszpan. They had a son, Hershel, who had somehow managed to escape in time to Paris to live with his uncle and aunt who had settled there earlier. From the moment that Hershel Grynszpan set foot in Paris and read in the French newspapers what was going on in that no-man's-land, he swore to become the avenger of his parents and all the Jewish people who were being so horribly abused by the Nazis.

On the morning of November 8, Hershel got hold of a gun, by means unknown, hid it under his raincoat and somehow gained entry into the German Consulate in Paris. He raced upstairs, entered one of the offices at random and shot the official on duty there. The victim's name was vom Rath who turned out later to have had no

Nazi affiliation. He was mortally wounded, but it took him a day and a half to die.

When Himmler and Goebbels realized that, unexpectedly, they had now come upon their rationale for unleashing their long-planned action against the Jews in Germany, Austria and Czechoslovakia, later dubbed the Crystal Night, they launched an unprecedented propaganda campaign inveighing against the "International Jewish Conspiracy" to destroy Germany even while they ordered their commandos of hoodlums into "spontaneous" action.

The Führer, who himself had been responsible for the mass murder of tens of thousands of his own countrymen, was so "distraught" about vom Rath that he rushed his personal physician to Paris to try to save his life, or perhaps to make sure that he wouldn't live. The fact is that vom Rath expired that very day.

While history is replete with examples of peoples' inability or refusal to recognize their enemies for what they are, suffering dire consequences as a result of their self-imposed amnesia, there are also impressive numbers of outstanding cases where people used their collective instincts to forestall some imminent disaster.

As those Jews, who by this time had not been able to get out from under the Nazi boot, were witnessing the crescendo of this trumped-up indignation about vom Rath's death, spewing forth from all outlets of the Nazi propaganda machine, they no longer had any doubt that something more horrible than anything in the horrible past was about to break loose and burst upon them.

One of the upshots of that recognition was an explosive intensification of correspondence going abroad, all pleading for help in getting out of that ever-tightening noose that was Nazi Germany.

While the response from abroad was pitifully inadequate to provide any long-term relief, the worldwide publication of these events helped in some measure to slow the momentum of the evil.

This was also true in the case of the next episode, the events of the Crystal Night.

TWENTY
The Kind Woods

It's been over fifty years now, the day was November 9, 1938, a bleak Wednesday, when I was one of a crowd of several hundred people that milled about on the dividing island of the *Friedberger Anlage* in the city of Frankfurt-on-Main, in front of the Great Synagogue. I was wearing blue working jeans, a pale-green imitation leather coat, a blue hat that working people used to wear then, and a pair of working boots. I was the only Jew in the crowd. The way I looked, it was unlikely that anybody would take me for Jewish. A few months earlier, another pseudo-Aryan pal of mine and I had boldly walked into a Nazi mass meeting in Hamburg where the district leader of "Germany North-West" was holding forth. Like everybody else, we stretched out our right arm after every second or third idiotic utterance by the speaker, as though we were just another pair of those witless robots that comprised the audience.

Tonight, however, was quite different. The Great Synagogue was being set on fire by a dozen or so hoodlums representing the hoodlum Führer of the German Reich. Within half an hour the building was fully ablaze and lit up the large plaza. The people's faces took on a deep red glow which accentuated their eyes to the point that they seemed to be popping out of their sockets. Everybody looked wild. They not only looked wild, they were wild. They were incredibly upset and some even felt so overwrought that they lost their composure and gave vent to their true feelings. I am sure if there had been an election, Hitler would not even have collected half of the one-third of the votes that he ever received prior to his appointment. Of course, after that, when they changed to open balloting supervised by bayonets, he raked in over 90 percent.

To say that the approval rate of the onlookers was minimal, is probably an understatement. I did not hear a single endorsement. The most frequent comment was, "Today the Jews, then it'll be us."

I was overcome by a blind rage, but the many cops and Gestapo that by now had arrived for "crowd control," would have made any overt act or even any sign of protest, suicidal.

That night this scene was replicated a thousand times in every German town, village or hamlet where there were any Jews left. It was not only the synagogues that were ruined but all the Jewish stores that had withstood a number of assaults in the past. Now they all had their windows smashed and were plundered.

It was at that time too that the Gestapo and SS began to pick up Jewish males, from fifteen to eighty, beating up many of them, killing those who resisted, and taking them to certain public buildings that had already been prepared for this purpose, notwithstanding Joseph Goebbels' insistence that these actions had all been spontaneous.

They registered the Jewish men, (these Germans are thorough!), and shipped them by truck or cattle cars to the nearest KZ, which term had become the gruesome German sobriquet for concentration camp. This action went on throughout the night, and for a whole week thereafter, the Gestapo and SS, in twos, threes and fours, went from house to house, from floor to floor, from apartment to apartment, from closet to closet, from train to train, rounding up all Jewish males that they could lay their hands on, except those who were sick in bed and had a doctor's certificate to prove it.

Naturally, the suicide rate among the Jews who did not have the stamina to endure this aggravated Nazi terror, climbed to an all-time high. It is impossible to describe that all-pervasive sense of doom and despair among the Jews. Quite a few non-Jewish Germans too who lost their cool and protested to these Nazi animals, found themselves in the same KZ as their Jewish neighbors.

When the Gestapo order to destroy the synagogues reached the Nazi mayor and party leader of my native village of Flieden, Hermann Heil, he gathered some of the local party faithfuls about him. They armed themselves with pickaxes and related paraphernalia to execute the order, and made for the synagogue.

According to the story that *Frau* Ida Link, a loyal friend of my mother's, told Carol and me about ten years after the war, not without considerable relish on her part and ours, she was watching from the front stoop of her house on the other side of the street as these goons were trying frantically to beat down the heavy oak entrance doors of the stone building, but to no avail. Suddenly, Mayor Heil took over, and in one gigantic lunge brought down his ax right on his left foot, cleaving it in two. I do not know how many religious people in the village regarded this accident as a sign from heaven, but it clearly saved the synagogue from destruction, and it stands to this day.

However, no more Jews live any longer in the village. Only their names engraved on the memorial stone slab in the now unused cemetery still bear mute witness to their former existence and their ultimate doom. The village of Flieden is now truly *judenrein*, or purged of Jews. On rare occasions a former Jewish resident or his descendant might come back, unobtrusively, for a whimsical afternoon trying to find his old family's house, or pay a visit to the grave of a relative at the cemetery, or to the synagogue, but he will rarely find what he came for. A different congregation has taken over the synagogue and they have erected a cross on the building's little steeple. They, unwittingly, have created a new link between the crucifixion and the holocaust.

Back in Frankfurt: After I had been watching this monstrous spectacle of the burning synagogue for a few hours, and had satisfied enough of my personal as well as collective masochistic needs, and had also watched most of the bedraggled crowd go home, I was overcome by an uncontrollable weariness and slowly made my way to the apartment of Levi and Röschen Stern on the *Sandweg*, about two hundred feet away. It had been only three days earlier that I had started my new job as an instructor of welding in the Jewish Training School in Frankfurt.

Alas, there was no permanence in this world of feverish change. I found the Sterns still awake, both in great distress, with tears running down their faces. Röschen Stern, who was Aunt Becka's sister, was known to let her nervousness out in streams of verbiage, while her husband Levi was known to be the silent type. We started to commiserate with one another, wondering whether this was the night when our ultimate fate would be sealed, until we were totally exhausted and went to bed.

It was almost 10 A.M. when I woke up. During those horrible times, I discovered that sleeping was the only means of preserving my sanity. When I entered the Stern's kitchen where Röschen was serving breakfast, I found that my good hosts were close to a nervous breakdown. After a period of almost unbearable silence, Röschen burst out with the remark, "Oh God, if they will find you here and take you away, I am going to die."

I realized that the atmosphere of this apartment had undergone a distinct change for the worse, to the point of becoming alarmingly contagious. I sensed that whatever my overall chances of escape might be, I was surely going to lose out if I were to stay with them even one more hour. I got my leather case which lately had become my best friend, and began to collect what under the existing circumstances appeared as the most vital commodity—underwear. Winter was near, and if I should wind up in one of those KZs, unheated as they were, undoubtedly without enough blankets to go around, good underwear was certain to be a vital item, although, nowadays, my former concern may evoke some injudicious giggling.

I had no compunctions borrowing two pairs of woolen long johns from Levi Stern, though he was making a long face. I knew that he had salvaged a bundle of those things when he sold their store.

I bade the Sterns a hearty good-bye and went down the elevator, and out through the glass-windowed front door. I saw a streetcar approach from the direction of the railroad station, and I ran toward it and jumped on it through the always open front door in order to get away from this dangerous hotspot in the city. At that moment, I looked furtively to the rear of the streetcar, and I thanked my lucky star for Röschen's hysterics, because at that very instant, I saw two SS men and one Gestapo jump off the back of the streetcar and enter the very apartment house where the Sterns lived and where I had been but a few seconds earlier.

Three weeks later, when that first big storm had blown over, I called the Sterns to thank them for their hospitality. They were overjoyed that I had survived this close encounter and all the other encounters that had occurred in the interim.

Dressed in my leather-imitation coat, my heavy work boots, and my blue cap, I jumped off the streetcar near the Panamanian Consulate. As I entered the waiting room, I sighted about fifty Jewish women of all ages crouched around the few available benches obviously in great distress and anxiety. When they noticed me they suspected me to be a Nazi official and a cry of great pain went up. I realized the situation and pointing to myself, reassured them that I was a Jew myself.

Besides the consul, officiating in an adjoining room, I was the only male person around. All these Jewish women had come to buy Panamanian visas for their husbands, sons, fathers, sweethearts, cousins, whoever had been caught in this Nazi razzia, for the rumor persisted that a visa to a foreign country could purchase a captive's early release from the KZ.

I do not remember why I was called into the consul's office ahead of all the other people, but I remember very well that the consul told me in somber words that going to Panama means also going to a difficult country, that physical labor was carried out by colored people only and that, therefore, I would not be able to do any welding there. I could not help making a mental note of the racism here and there. Besides, he added regretfully, he had just received a telegram advisory from the foreign ministry of Panama that he was not to issue anymore visas to people who had the intention of actually migrating to Panama for the visas would not be honored.

However, he could continue to issue visas for the inmates of concentration camps to get them released, provided they won't try to use them. With that I purchased two such visas for DM 35 each, one for my sister Elli's husband, Siegmund Lowenstein, and another for my then fiancée Carol's brother, Menko Lomnitz, who were respectively in the KZs of Buchenwald and Dachau.

After the transaction, the consul called me back to his office and, to my surprise, handed me his business card with the address and telephone number of his private residence on it inviting me to call on him if I ever needed any help. I expressed my deep-felt gratitude to him and left. It was something like the proverbial silver lining on this dark cloud of the fascist horizon.

It was almost noontime, when I arrived back at the training school. I found a debate was going on among the small group of instructors of whom I was one, as to whether it was wiser for everybody to leave the building at once and try his luck individually, or to stay together and face whatever should happen to us as a group.

I soon realized that the majority of these people who were all about my age, were in favor of staying in this mousetrap and awaiting their certain fate in unity, as their "duty" dictated. I, on the other hand, felt their reasoning unacceptable. I argued that if we split, students and all, at least some of us might have a chance to slip through the Nazi web, and that I saw no reason at all to accommodate those Nazi bastards and let them catch us all in a heap like a bunch of witless sheep. In any case, I would not stay.

With that, I picked up my leather case, wished everybody good luck and went downstairs. I opened the heavy door and stepped outside trying to figure out my immediate itinerary. However, I did not have to bother. For just a couple of hundred feet to my right, I saw and heard a howling mob of more than a hundred people milling toward our school. I immediately turned to the left, turned left again, and reached the Main Kay. One block from there to the right, was one of the bridges over the Main River, leading to the town of Sachsenhausen, where very few Jews lived, and where, therefore, the Nazis could be expected to be less rampant, and that is where I turned now.

I learned later that within minutes, all the others in the school, instructors and students alike, were seized in a body and shipped to the KZ.

Once across the bridge, I walked on and on, up a long hill, until I finally came to the end of town. To the left, there was a wooded section, and I thought that I could perhaps find a hiding place there. It was a forest of large leaf trees spaced at fairly regular intervals, but there was not much underbrush for an easy hiding place. After awhile, I found a tree in the center of a circle of trees that would allow me to notice anybody approaching while I would enjoy a fair safeguard against surprise. Besides, I was so exhausted that I could hardly have gone any further.

As I was settling down at that tree, it occurred to me that the weather was unusually mild for that time of year, but the sky was clouded over and I felt that there might be some rain soon. Before another minute passed, I had fallen into a sound sleep.

I slept peacefully through the night and I awoke at the crack of dawn, still leaning against the tree. The clouds were still there and there was a whiff of rain in the air. I decided to wait till noon. Then I would take a chance and get something to eat, for I had not eaten or drunk anything for the last twenty hours. I went back down that long hill and with studied nonchalance, walked into the first pub on the way.

The barkeep was talking to two men sitting at the bar. When I entered, they turned toward me to get a bead on me. I casually raised my right arm halfway, without adding the usual "Heil Hitler," and sat down at one of three tables. Luckily, they had a warm soup on their meager menu. The barkeep came over to me, and I gave him my order. The men continued their conversation in a low voice, but it was obvious that they were discussing the most acute question of the day, the one that overshadowed all others, the Nazi manhunt of the Jews. Periodically, they turned toward me. Did they suspect my being Jewish, or was I just a stranger in the pub, in which case they had to be doubly careful with their conversation?

As soon as I finished, I paid and left. On the way back to "my" tree I picked up the *Frankfurter Zeitung*, so that I could have at least some information of what was going on in this cauldron. I also picked up some bread, a few bananas and a bottle of seltzer for my supper and perhaps my breakfast too.

After I had settled down again in my hiding place, I looked at the newspaper. Although the *Frankfurter Zeitung* was the sole survivor of the great liberal tradition of German journalism, paradoxically, as a protégé of the *I.G. Farben* in their eagerness to keep their foreign customers in good humor, it nonetheless had to be very careful not to step on Dr. Goebbels' sensitive toes.

There were indeed several perfunctory reports in the newspaper about the "spontaneous" action by the German people to avenge themselves against the "crime" against the German nation committed by a Jew in Paris against a member of the German delegation. It all sounded very innocent and stood no comparison with the real thing.

Not only *I.G. Farben*, but the Nazis too hoped that by keeping this pseudo-liberal newspaper alive, they could score some Brownie points with their friends abroad, for their foreign trade was hurting. It was a bitter irony that the same *I.G. Farben*, once Hitler started the actual shooting war, were held harmless for losing their world-wide markets by engineering, installing and maintaining the gas chambers and ovens in such illustrious centers of German culture as Auschwitz, Treblinka, Maidanek, etc. and, thereby, became one of the most profitable German enterprises.

My mind drifted to other subjects. Of course, the human cattle drive that was going on just a couple of miles from where I was hiding and throughout the entire country was the most persistently intrusive

105

object in this kaleidoscope of horrors. Where I was, it felt like the silent eye of a raging storm.

I had always been interested in history. During the five years of being a leader in the Zionist youth movement, I constantly had to expand my historic knowledge, particularly Jewish history, in order to lecture on these subjects, sometimes on short notice.

There was no dearth of tragic events in the three and a half millennia of Jewish history.

Perhaps the saddest event occurred upon the death of the great King Solomon, when his arrogant son, Rehobeam, so enraged the elders that the realm split into the ten and a half tribes of Israel and the two and one-half tribes of Judea. The division into two separate states made each one extremely vulnerable to attack and would, within three hundred years, lead to the destruction and complete disappearance of Israel, while the more compact state of Judea managed to withstand another one hundred fifty years of almost relentless onslaughts by hostile neighbors, before the Judeans too were subdued and exiled to Babylonia for half a century until the generous Persian emperor, Cyrus, let them return.

A second period of bloodletting of the Jewish people began during their war of rebellion against the Roman Empire in the years A.D. 66 to A.D. 70. In the end, after one million Jews had starved and bled to death, Titus, the son and successor of the Flavian emperor Vespasian, transported countless tens of thousands of Jewish captives to Rome, men and women, young and old and, yoked together, made them pass in shame under the triumphal arch that bears his name. He then forced them to build the Roman Colosseum during the ensuing decade between A.D. 70 and A.D. 80.

Many of those laborers refused to be treated as slaves and ran away, building a city under the city of Rome. Here they lived, married, had children, died and were buried. For a total length of twenty miles, they set up a network of apartments, often five stories deep. They had their own administration. They established relations with other Jewish colonies, notably among them Alexandria in Egypt, where a half million Jews lived. When the Alexandrian Jews rose up against Rome under the leadership of Bar Kochba, many underground people in Rome became partisans to their brethren in Egypt. They even enticed the emperor's mistress, Berenice, the beautiful sister of the King Herod Agrippa, to subsidize their cause. They also organized migration into outposts of the Roman Empire such as Spain, Southern France, the Rhineland, Northern Africa and the lands of the Levante. It was only during the sunset of the Roman Empire in the fifth century that the Roman Jews blended into the landscape and were almost totally assimilated in the mix of Greek, Germanic, Gallic, North African and even Phoenician elements.

However, by that time, new Jewish centers had arisen. Foremost among them was the Jewish community in Spain, in the Christian as well as the Moslem sections.

Cities like Cordova, Toledo, Sevilla and Segovia, names such as Maimonides, Judah ben Halevy, Solomon ibn Gabirol, Moses ibn Ezra, Samuel Ha-Nagid, are but a few of the most prominent among the shining lights from that golden age of Spain, the mere mention of which, even nowadays, is apt to send a collective shiver down the spines of a Jewish audience.

How sad that the feudal forces of darkness, secular and clerical, decided to do away with this incredibly rich growth of Jewish as well as Moslem middle class culture, a gross act of self-immolation for Spain, as it turned out to be for centuries to come.

What a terrible time of deprivation those refugees had to endure! Often, their ship's captain was in cahoots with pirates. The whole sordid lot of passengers was killed for their possessions or sold into slavery, waiting to be ransomed by their brethren.

The expulsion of the Jews from Spain resulted in an even wider spread of the Diaspora. Besides Holland, Turkey, and North Africa, Jews went as far as India, China and Japan, even to Brazil, truly to the four ends of the earth. It was during this man-made cataclysm that my own forefathers were tossed about in history's unpredictable storms and perforce wound up in Holland before they settled in Germany. Of course Spain was not the only land of misery for the Jews. In the east, in Poland and the Ukraine, the Jews were originally welcome and they attained a high cultural level after their migration from central Europe during the centuries of the crusades, the plagues, of death and deprivation. In the east, their first encounter with the bitter sting of persecution occurred at the end of the Thirty Years' War. The Cossacks, which were being used by the Russian aristocracy as a sort of mobile mercenary force to conquer new feudal lands for them, ransacked the Polish countryside and in the process destroyed a great number of Jewish communities and killed perhaps as many as half a million Jews.

The tsars of Russia, the kings of Poland, and above all, the beleaguered Catholic Church, were quick in adopting this strategy for their own unholy ends and right up to the end of the Russian Revolution, they would routinely hire these sanguinary bands of Cossacks to do their dirty work and kill all their enemies, real or imagined. That is why there was hardly ever a period without serious bloodshed visited upon the Jews in those countries.

One of the worst of such massacres occurred toward the end of the Russo-Japanese War in 1905, when a horde of crazed Cossacks under the leadership of a killer named Petljura, went on a bloody rampage in the Ukraine and murdered many thousands of Jews.

A young Jewish boy by the name of Joseph Schwarzbart, watched the massacre of his own family and his community by Petljura and his gang from a hiding place in the woods. Twenty years later, after he had migrated to Paris he spotted this same Petljura sipping away at a cup of tea at one of the fashionable outdoor cafes on one of the Parisian boulevards. The Cossack leader was but one of many Russian émigrés who had good reasons to flee the revolution. Schwarzbart quickly helped himself to a gun and shot Petljura dead, right where he was sitting.

Schwarzbart was apprehended immediately, but when he told his story in a French court, the jury pronounced him not guilty.

As these cruel episodes depicting centuries of history were flashing through my mind, I could not help evolving some close association with several of those events. As a matter of fact, the vision of the Schwarzbart lad hiding in the woods jolted me right back to reality. Did history not repeat itself time and again?

But the time of reminiscing did not end here. I was now thinking of my own family members. Of course, my brother Theo, right after marrying Elsie Heim, had left for America and that way he had eluded the present dragnet. But my older brother Julius was still in Fulda, and I was wondering whether they had caught him. Carol's younger brother had also managed to get to America. Her second brother lived in Paris, France, but her older brother Menko was in the KZ of Dachau. Of course, my dear sister Elli's husband, Siegmund Lowenstein was in the KZ of Buchenwald.

I had given those two Panamanian visas to Carol to send one by express mail to my sister Elli, and the other to her own father so they could take them to their local police headquarters for processing in order to have the two men released from the KZ.

These were some of my thoughts before I treated myself to supper. If only it wouldn't rain.

Nature, however, ignored my wishful thinking. The clouds were thickening and I had to consider leaving my sylvan abode though I had absolutely no idea where to go. I was sure of one thing, namely that I would not voluntarily surrender to the attitude of self-effacement that the Nazi propaganda machine had so cleverly induced among the entire German people that they, for the most part, obediently submitted to their masters.

The notion that 90 percent of the Germans were of poor Aryan stock, while the Ruhr barons, the big bankers and, above all, the Nazi leadership, were supposed to represent the high-quality Aryans, was simplistic, preposterous and transparent to many. This realization hardened my resolve to make every effort not to get caught in this insane manhunt.

I waited till it was dark. It still had not started to rain and I stayed in my hideout a few hours longer. Then at nine o'clock I felt the first poky rain drops. I packed my belongings in my leathercase, and started to walk down that same long hilly road that had brought me to my refuge in the first place. After a half hour of walking, I came upon a huge plaza. At the northeast corner I found a public telephone. I called Elsie's aunt and asked her whether they could accommodate me for the night. Surprisingly, she invited me to her house without the least hesitation.

As I started to cross the plaza a stentorian voice behind me, that could only belong to a policeman, called out to me "Halt!" I kept walking as though I had not heard the order to stop and he again barked "Halt!" Once again, I pretended not to hear him and, wonder of wonders, he did not repeat his command a third time, nor did he make an attempt to apprehend me or ask for identification. Although I did not dare turn around to look, the sound of his boots told me that he was walking away in the opposite direction.

The only explanation that I can give for this behavior is that he must have been a decent person. After having gone through the motions of trying to stop me, as was his duty to do, he decided that he really did not want to go through with it after all.

After crossing the nearby Main bridge, it took me almost another hour to reach the elegant apartment in a patrician house at the other end of town where the Bruchfelds, Elsie's aunt and uncle, lived. It was a district where many rich Jews lived.

Elsie's uncle was in bed. He told me that he had a certificate from his doctor, that he was ill and bedridden. For a few minutes we exchanged the latest news, the latest atrocities as it were, and Claire showed me to my bedroom. Soon I slept the sleep of the just.

Again, I awoke early and got dressed. The atmosphere during breakfast was much more composed than at the Sterns. However, *Herr* Bruchfeld was noticeably preoccupied with the validity of his medical certificate, whether it would stand up when the inevitable Gestapo visit came. Probably the SS won't give a damn at all and push it aside as long as a guy could stand on his legs.

He went back to his bed and sure enough, within a few minutes the doorbell rang. I hid behind the door and Claire, waving the doctor's certificate in her hand, went to open the door and squeezed out a courageous "Yes?" "Who lives here?" an officious sounding Gestapo man (who else?) asked. "Well, my husband and myself, and he is sick," was her brave answer. "Nobody else living here?" "No, nobody else," she lied, but it worked. They left without coming in and I was safe. However, this brief encounter with destiny had a traumatic effect on *Herr* Bruchfeld.

As though he was now trying to emulate Röschen Stern, he suddenly cried out that he would surely not survive if they were to find me in their house the next time around. It was clear that Elsie's Tante Claire had by far the better nerves.

Again, for the sake of preserving my sanity, I decided to take off. After thanking them for their kindness, I went downstairs and exited the house through a wrought iron gate. At that moment of despair as to what I should do next, I suddenly remembered the "invitation" I had received from the Panamanian consul and I turned left to reach his residence.

A footnote: About three weeks later, when I met the Bruchfelds again, Tante Claire seemed shocked when she saw me. She told me excitedly that it had been but a couple of minutes after I had left their apartment when a whole gang of Nazis broke into their house and searched every nook and cranny for escapees. She had been absolutely certain that they had caught me as I was leaving their house. Strangely, I had not noticed anything.

I had to walk cross-town for nearly two hours, until I reached the house of the Panamanian consul shortly after 1 P.M., Saturday. An indistinct apartment complex in one of the lesser sections of town, the nameplate pointed to an apartment on the second floor. It was dark inside and I had trouble finding the doorbell. A heavyset woman opened the door and I explained to her how I came to be there at this time. She became testy and said that the consul was not home, and she would not let me enter their apartment.

At this point I was too desperate to give up and I asked her if she would not at least let me sit down for a few minutes since I was really exhausted from my long walk. After some more talking, she softened and allowed me ten minutes to rest up.

After awhile, she came back and brought me a plate of hot pea soup and I knew that I had broken the ice. She now was a changed person. After a lengthy conversation about the state of the world, and that of Frankfurt in particular, the consul came home. He was very nice and handed me an application for Panama. Although the immigration into Panama was still officially closed, he thought that they might resume granting visas fairly soon and in that case he would submit my application right away.

Mindful of his somber warning a few days earlier, about the inappropriateness of white people doing manual labor in Panama, I took great care in filling out the application. I thanked him for everything and I also thanked his wife for the soup and left.

Throughout all these days of unmitigated horror, I had managed to stay in telephone contact with Carol, my fiancée. While I could not use Stern's or Bruchfeld's phone, because one had to assume that they were bugged, there were public phones everywhere.

Even while I had been waiting for the consul to come home, I had conceived of a plan of escape that might work. As it were, I had no alternative. First, I called Carol from a public telephone and asked her whether I could stay for the night at the orphanage where she was a nurse and where her cousin was the headmistress.

She answered that her cousin had given strict instructions not to harbor any refugees, but that this Saturday, she had taken off for the rest of the day and that they could smuggle me in. Even if she were to find out the next morning, so what?

It took me about one and a half hours to reach the orphanage where Carol and her friend Lore were waiting for me. They huddled me away to an unused room. Later, when bedtime came, they prepared a small child's bed on the children's ward on the second floor and put a pair of infant shoes in front of it. I bedded down, somewhat cramped, pulled a sheet over my head and fell asleep instantly.

It was about six o'clock in the morning when I awoke with a start. There was knocking at the main door. Carol and Lore rushed down "to meet the enemy." At the same time they told one of the young girls who was with them to wake me up and show me the way out of the rear of the building. Since I had taken the precaution of not undressing for the night, it took me just a few seconds to collect my good friend, the leathercase, and get out through the rear door and jump over a stone wall into an adjoining garden.

In less than a half hour, Carol called me back, and told me that the Gestapo had only been there for a routine check on food and provisions in the orphanage and that her cousin, the headmistress, had returned and somehow had found out about me, and she was furious, but that she was already starting to calm down.

At ten o'clock, Carol called up my brother Theo's father-in-law who lived in a small village thirty miles from Frankfurt. Elsie's father, Isidor Heim, still a handsome man of about fifty, walked with a slight limp. He was an invalid from the First World War, and as such was the only male Jew in the Hessian village of Crumstadt, who had not been picked up and taken to a KZ. Therefore, since everyone else had been accounted for, no further searches were expected there and it looked like an ideal place for me to hide.

Herr Heim was agreeable and told Carol that he expected "Bertha" on the five o'clock train, at which time it would be quite dark already and that he would be at the station and guide me to his house, but that I should keep a safe distance from him.

Once again, I was lucky. When I came to the Frankfurt railroad station, I saw many Gestapo and SS men, but they were only working the long-distance trains. Except for the regular train conductor to punch my ticket, it looked like a good omen that I saw nobody else in uniform during my hour-long train ride to Crumstadt.

When the train stopped in Crumstadt, only two other people got out of the train with me. Sure enough, there stood *Herr* Heim on the other side of the road, leaning against his bicycle. As soon as he recognized me he got on his bike and, keeping my distance, I followed him to his house where his wife Dinah was waiting for us. It was only a few days later, that I learned how lucky I had really been getting out of Frankfurt in time. For that Monday morning that followed my Sunday afternoon trip to Crumstadt, the Nazis had evolved a new strategy, far more efficient than their earlier, more haphazard method. Now they encircled entire city blocks and, block by block, sent large contingents of men into every house on that block, and this dragnet ruled out any escape. Maybe I had developed a hunted animal's instinct.

Isidor Heim showed me to my room on the second floor. I was to stay there all the time with the window curtains drawn except when called down to eat. They also advised me that in no event was I to use the outhouse during the daylight hours.

Dinah Heim had prepared a most delicious meal, perhaps with a little more garlic than I cared for, but for the first time in a week, I felt almost like a normal human being again.

Since the house stood in the center of a large fenced-in courtyard, it was safe to be listening to some of my favorite foreign radio stations, such as Strasbourg, London and Moscow. Their newscasts helped us considerably to keep our sanity.

As a bona fide war veteran, *Herr* Heim could circulate fairly freely in the village. Besides doing the necessary shopping, he would also get the local newspaper and bring it to me.

I stayed in Crumstadt for two weeks until the fever heat in Frankfurt and elsewhere began to recede somewhat and the Nazis gradually released most of their recent Jewish prisoners from the KZs regardless of whether they had visas. Some came back to their families in coffins with the terse explanation that they had been shot while trying to escape. To the recipients of such gruesome freight, it became obvious that they had been clubbed to death. On the whole it seemed that the numerous protests from abroad against the incarceration and maltreatment of the Jews had given the Nazi leaders some second thoughts, and they decided to call this idiotic stunt off, at least for the time being.

I went back to Fulda by train, and found that my brother Julius had been imprisoned in the local jail for three days, after which they set him free. My sister-in-law, Bella, told me that the Fulda police chief, Berend, whose son used to be a friend of my brother Theo's, had called up four times during those critical three weeks, telling her each time that he had just dispatched the Gestapo to our house to pick me up. That was nice of him. He did not know that all that time I had not been home in Fulda, anyway.

TWENTY-ONE
Salvation

Every one of my instincts told me that this reprieve from terror would be of short duration, and I began the strongest efforts to get out of the Nazi inferno. Of course, my preference was still Palestine, but when I found that the few permits for Palestine that the British handed out in those critical days, were all gobbled up by the big shots of our Zionist Youth Movement in Berlin, I started to send out all sorts of desperate letters and applications to England, Australia and the United States. I even applied for immigration into Honduras and Nicaragua, not to forget Panama. The hour of the daily mail delivery became the tensest time of the day. For a long time, it was also the most frustrating.

Because my brother Theo had also been trying to help the family members still in Germany from his new country, the United States of America, and for that reason had been in touch with a distant relative in London, our new contact person, I quite unexpectedly received a permit for England on April 15, 1939, a Saturday. Since Carol had left for England just a fortnight earlier, the receipt of my English permit proved doubly fortuitous. I recalled that on the day of her departure when I had seen her off at the train station in Frankfurt and we kissed each other farewell, we both had the terrible foreboding that we would never see each other again.

With the receipt of the English permit, of course, the decision to leave Naziland had been made for me, but in the end, I went away only with the most serious misgivings. I would have to leave behind my good mother, my brother Julius and his family, my beloved sister Elli and her family, and Carol's parents, not to speak of some dear friends of mine. In retrospect, I realize that my premonitions regarding their fate when all hell would break loose, were justified to a devastating degree.

As for myself, I decided to lose no time. That same afternoon, I went to the railroad station in Fulda and bought my tickets to London, England, via Holland. You will remember that it was then that I had a brief encounter with my good friend Albert. The next Monday morning, I went to see *Herr* Berend at the police headquarters in Fulda and, armed with the English entrance permit and the tickets, I applied for a passport. Due to the friendship between my brother Theo and Berend's son, it took just two days before I received my German passport. I took notice that the issuers of my passport had provided me with the middle name of Israel, in accordance with a recent directive by Dr. Goebbels, the purveyor of a warped sense of humor, although I realized that this intended slur would come to an unlamented end as soon as I entered England. Waiting for the passport gave me a chance to do my "packing." I had already set aside a box made of plywood reinforced by a frame of aluminum angles. I had to decide what I could dare include in this box, considering that the Nazis would probably make me open it in order to inspect the contents before I crossed the border. In addition, I had a leather suitcase which contained my everyday needs as well as an extra set of underwear while my documents and personal papers went into the leathercase, my faithful friend from my days in the woods.

I also took a train to Fritzlar to see my sister Elli. It was obvious that she had set all her hopes for her and her family's rescue on my going to England.

Taking for granted that an application for her and her family to go to England had been made by my brother Theo's contact in London and was under imminent consideration by the British Home Office, I promised her that I would do everything I could to hasten her coming to England. It was five tearful decades later on a trip to Germany that I finally found out that she, her husband Siegmund, and their darling boy Bernd, were all shot dead in the Kaiserwald, near Riga, and were buried in a mass grave.

Our dear mother contracted pneumonia just a couple of days before she was to leave from Hamburg for the United States and died the very day that the *USS Constitution*, on which we had booked her passage, sailed into New York harbor.

Carol's beloved parents, Joseph and Sophie Lomnitz, were taken to the Teresienstadt Camp and perished there within three months of their arrival. I know now that man's inability to look into the future is one of nature's most magnanimous blessings, indeed.

Early Monday morning, I took a train to Frankfurt to obtain an official release from the district tax office that cleared me of any and all tax obligations toward the Reich and, the following afternoon, a Tuesday, April 18, 1939, I crossed the sandy no-man's-land of the German-Dutch border near Venlo.

To watch the dour German border guards leave the train at Venlo Station and the warmly smiling Dutch customs people take their place was a totally indescribable experience. As I left the sands of sorrow behind me, I felt like a giant reborn.